Up in all Weather

The Story of RAF Docking

David Jacklin

Larks Press

Published by the Larks Press
Ordnance Farmhouse
Guist Bottom, Dereham
01328 829207

Printed by Newprint and Design,
Garrood Drive, Fakenham,
Norfolk.
01328 851578

First published May 2004
Reprinted 2005, 2009

British Library Cataloguing-in-Publication-Data
A catalogue record for this book is available
from the British Library

A full catalogue of Larks Press books is available at
www.booksatlarkspress.co.uk

About the Author

David Jacklin is a former Royal Air Force Squadron Leader, who was actively involved in the training of RAF officers and technicians. After his RAF career, David worked with NATO for twenty years at the Supreme Headquarters Allied Powers Europe (SHAPE) in Belgium, where he was employed as a senior systems engineer.

David was born in Norfolk, spending some of his childhood living on the ex-RAF camp near Sunderland Farm outside the village of Docking. Later his family moved into the village, where he spent the remainder of his childhood, receiving his education at local schools in Docking, Hunstanton and King's Lynn. He later joined the Royal Air Force as a Halton apprentice in the late 1950s.

David is an experienced software engineer and technical teacher possessing a Bachelor of Science honours degree and a Post Graduate certificate in Education.

He is now retired, living with his wife near Diss on the Norfolk/Suffolk border. He may be reached by telephone on 01379 741884 or by email at djacklin@aol.com.

ISBN 978 1 904006 19 1

Author's Acknowledgements

I am particularly grateful for the personal recollections provided by several generous people who either flew from Docking, served at Docking in a non-flying capacity or knew the wartime airfield well as civilians:

The late Mr Les Hart, an ex RAF pilot of 519 and 521 squadrons, kindly provided photographs and written accounts of meteorological sorties to and from Docking, including a Ventura aircraft crash on the airfield. Mr Bill Davis, now at Happisburgh in Norfolk, served as wireless operator/air gunner with 521 Squadron, flying from Bircham Newton and Docking. He kindly supplied photographs and an extract from his wartime diaries. Mr Frank Goff, an ex-pilot with 206 Squadron and 279 Squadron, who now lives at Salhouse in Norfolk, kindly lent his pilot's flying log books, photographs and other material covering his time at Bircham Newton and Docking. Mr Jack Allaway, an ex-navigator from 521 Squadron, provided details of his horrific crash during take-off from Docking in 1943. He also shared some of his memories of wartime Docking.

Mr Derek Small, an ex-RAF navigator who was trained in Canada, who now lives in Harleston, Norfolk, was kind enough to discuss his time at Docking with the future actors Richard Burton, Mick Misell (Warren Mitchel) and Tim Hardy (Robert Hardy).

Mr John Lucas, from Deal in Kent, who served in the Flying Control and Motor Transport sections at RAF Docking, kindly shared his memories of driving the ambulance to rush injured personnel to the parent station for medical attention.

Three ex-WAAFs who served at Docking made a large contribution to this book. Mrs Ellen Finch of Stanhoe was kind enough to retell her wartime experiences serving at Docking. Mrs Doris Driver, from Great Massingham, and Mrs Dorothy Jackson, from Finedon in Northamptonshire, also discussed their shared wartime memories of Docking, supplying photographs for inclusion in this book.

Several local civilians also contributed to this book. Mr Alan Watts and Mr Tony Arter of Docking kindly shared their experiences visiting the airfield as young men. Tony also provided historical photographs of Docking village. Mr Derek Rolfe, who now lives in Canada, provided information about air experience flights provided to ATC cadets. Mr Robert Perowne of High House Farm gave me access to the land around Sunderland Farm to take photographs of the present day airfield. He also supplied historical material and early photographs of the post-war Docking airfield.

A former Docking girl, Mrs Doris Rumbellow, who now lives nearby at Heacham, kindly shared her wartime memories of life on Lugden Hill Farm. Finally, Mr Colin Coe of Lower Farm, Bircham, shared his memories of visiting RAF Docking during WW2.

I am very grateful for the help given by Mr Peter B. Gunn from Docking, author of a recent book, called 'Bircham Newton –A Norfolk Airfield in War and Peace'. Peter carefully read a draft of my book and offered many helpful suggestions and also supplied an interesting Location Plan of Docking, which is included in the first chapter. I have tried, where possible, to ensure that this book about RAF Docking complements Peter's book about RAF Bircham Newton. However, since the two books were researched independently, some duplication has inevitably occurred.

During my research I consulted various Operations Records Books and other RAF documents held at the Public Records Office in Kew and several published books, which are listed below with my grateful appreciation to the authors. I would particularly like to acknowledge that items 1 to 4 and item 14 of the Bibliography provide good summaries of WW2 operations at Docking, which were used as the starting point for my research.

CONTENTS

Surviving concrete perimeter track at Docking

Prologue

'That old airfield and its buildings remain rooted in my memory.'

Shortly after the Second World War, when I was a young boy, I lived with my family in ex-RAF hutments that had been part of RAF Docking. At that time, in the late 1940s, the RAF station was no longer operational, but was being used by the local council as temporary civilian housing to help overcome post-war shortages. The huts, which had been RAF and WAAF barracks, were very basic, being made of a wood and plaster board. The thin exterior walls were covered in a black material, similar to present day roofing felt, which gave them quite a sinister appearance. The roof of each hut was constructed from a grey asbestos material. Inside there were several bedrooms interlinked via a long corridor and, at one end of each hut, there was an anteroom. This room, which was the only one possessing any heating, in the form of a coal-burning stove, became our living room. I remember that all the floors were covered in brown linoleum. The huts had no electricity, so paraffin lamps and candles were used for lighting. They did not even possess mains water. A daily chore involved filling up pails of water from a shared outside tap, which was fed from a nearby military-styled galvanized water tank, supported by a gantry of metal struts and legs called a Braithwaite Tower. This was a local landmark that could be seen for miles around.

Not that we noticed these austere conditions; we were just happy to live and play in such an extraordinary environment,

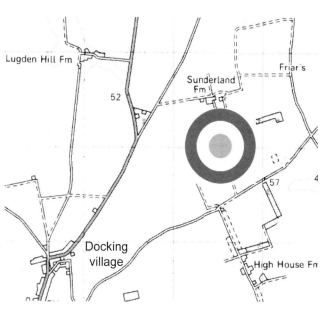

with abandoned military buildings for us to explore and enjoy. One particular favourite was the air-raid shelter in our garden. All that was visible above ground was a grass mound, which hid the underground concrete structure, designed to give protection against enemy bombs. To gain entrance to the shelter one had to

1

descend a flight of steps, which gave access to the cylindrical-shaped concrete interior. At the opposite end to the entrance steps there was an emergency exit, consisting of a small covered hatch, which was accessed by climbing up a metal ladder. However, to our fertile young imaginations the shelter could be a dungeon, a submarine, or whatever we wanted it to be. Several minor injuries resulted from tumbles down the concrete steps or falls from the escape ladder. Eventually, our parents had to place the shelter out of bounds. However, this wasn't considered too much of a hardship, since there were many more buildings in which to play.

There were three types of empty huts in the vicinity: the previously-mentioned plasterboard hutments of the type that my family lived in, which were called Laing huts; Nissen huts made from sheets of corrugated metal bolted together to give a semi-circular cross section; and small brick buildings coated in concrete, called Maycrete huts. One of the Nissen huts was occasionally used as a Sunday school, since the village church and chapel were some distance away. I remember that we all had to take our own chairs along and that we self-consciously attempted to sing hymns, mostly out of tune. Some of the Maycrete huts were on another site alongside the main road from Docking to Brancaster, much closer to the village of Docking, not far from the railway station. These huts were also occupied as temporary housing in the post-war years. To differentiate between the two occupied sites, local people called them the 'near' huts or the 'far' huts, referring to their relative distance from the village.

Near a junction on the Docking to Brancaster road, about a mile or so outside the village, there was another RAF site, called the Communal Site, containing more substantial buildings. One of these larger buildings appeared to us to be an old hospital. It was very dark and ghostly inside this building and we always thought that it was haunted or occupied by tramps and vagabonds. Consequently, we would only enter the building as an act of extreme bravado, to satisfy a dare or a bet. To my great surprise, I later learned that it had been a gas decontamination centre.

All the RAF personnel had departed from Docking by the time we arrived on the scene, although we frequently met American airmen, who had begun to occupy the former RAF airfield of Sculthorpe, situated a few miles away. The Americans were very generous, and we soon learned that a shout of 'Got any gum, chum?' was usually rewarded with a stick of chewing gum.

In retrospect, it is apparent that we had few luxuries in our lives. Everything appeared to be rationed and many things were scarce. Many of the families cultivated large vegetable gardens and kept chickens to help supplement their meagre rations. To save a long walk into the village for shopping, local trades-men visited the site selling groceries, bread, bottled drink, and other essentials. I Pbelieve that milk and eggs could also be purchased from Sunderland Farm nearby.

The one luxury that we did enjoy was a daily ride to the local primary school in a taxi, which was a large wooden-trimmed shooting brake driven by a charming local woman, known to us all as Miss Dobbie. If we missed this taxi service, it was quite a long walk to the school, more than three miles away. One walking route to school took us past the water tower and along a track to the farmhouse and a large black hangar before passing quite close to an abandoned control tower and around a concrete perimeter track, which circled the old grass airstrip belonging to RAF Docking. It was impossible for a small boy to view this scene without

The author with siblings in the late 1940s

imagining what it would have been like three or four years before, when the country was at war. There would have been the throbbing sounds of heavy aircraft engines and other noisy activities associated with refuelling and bombing up the aircraft and getting them airborne. So it wasn't too difficult for me to imagine the roar of these engines and to see the aircraft climbing into the sky. I could even enter an old brick gun post and shoot down imaginary aircraft, or descend into an old air raid shelter to escape from make-believe bombs. Many a dream was hatched on that long dawdle to or from school. Needless to say, I was often late for morning assembly.

The locals called the RAF station 'Sunderland' because it was located so close to Sunderland Farm. However, to the families that lived in those temporary ex-RAF hutments, it was simply called 'the huts'. Most of the families, including my own, were re-housed in the village of Docking by the early 1950s. An era had passed, but that old airfield and its buildings remain rooted in my memory.

I left Docking in the late 1950s to pursue my own RAF career, which was followed by a second career working as a civilian for NATO in Belgium. When I returned to England in the late 1990s, I made a nostalgic visit to my childhood playground near Sunderland Farm. As expected, most of the buildings belonging to the former airfield at RAF Docking had been dismantled and the land returned to agriculture. Sadly, what remains of the airfield and its buildings is in a dilapidated state. Slowly, but surely, the forces of man and nature are reclaiming the area. Only an old, windowless control tower and a few decaying buildings remain as defiant monuments to past glories. Soon there will be nothing left to identify the former airfield and remind us of its past.

3

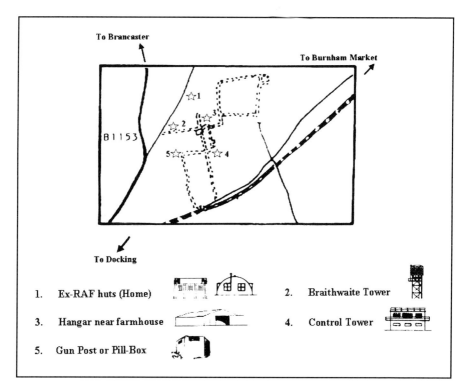

My memory of the airfield with some of the familiar buildings

Docking's war, and the brave exploits of its airmen and airwomen, went largely unpublished at the time, and little has been written about it since. Many airmen who lost their lives flying operations from Docking and its parent station, or who crashed in the local area, are interred in local churchyards. Many more were shot down over the North Sea and have watery graves. A visit to the local war graves, particularly those at St Mary's Church at Great Bircham, will provide a poignant reminder of the scale of wartime operations and the huge loss of life around this corner of west Norfolk.

The purpose of this book is to record some of the wartime exploits of the flying squadrons, airmen and airwomen that served at RAF Docking before they are lost to future generations. It is dedicated to their memory, particularly to those who made the ultimate sacrifice.

Lest we forget

DAVID JACKLIN
Diss, Norfolk
January, 2003

4

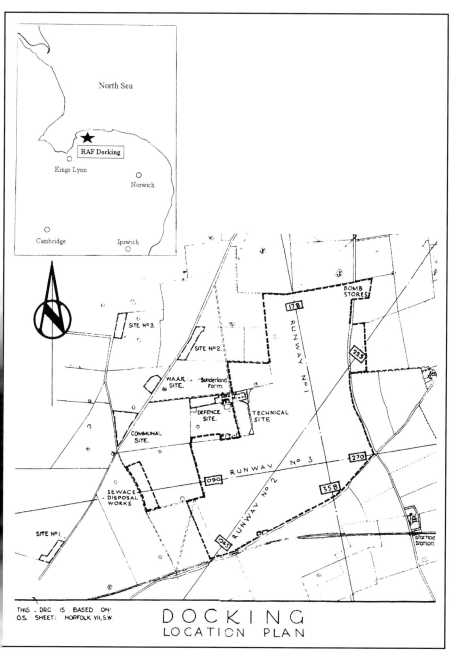

Wartime Docking Location Plan

1. Overview of Docking Airfield and Operations

'Perhaps Docking's greatest contribution to the war effort was in the field of meteorological reconnaissance.'

Most of the derelict Norfolk airfield of RAF Docking is located about two miles outside the village in a north-east direction, east of the B1154 road leading out of Docking towards Brancaster. About a mile and a half from the village, there is a fork in this road where a smaller road leads off towards Brancaster Staithe. Many of the original buildings were located near this road junction. The former airfield, which consisted of grass runways and concrete perimeter tracks, is due east of the junction, in a south-east direction from Sunderland Farm.

This wartime map shows the location of the airfield and the roads mentioned in the text. The first site, labelled SITE No 1, which contained RAF quarters, is shown at the bottom left-hand corner of the map, on the left-hand side of the Brancaster road. This was the closest site to the village, just a few hundred yards from the railway station. Like the huts mentioned in the introduction, these buildings were also used as emergency civilian housing after the war.

Some of the more substantial buildings, including the airmen's dining room, NAAFI, officers' mess, sergeants' mess and a gas decontamination centre, were near the first fork in the road. This is labelled COMMUNAL SITE on the map. The author also remembers that a water reservoir, resembling a small swimming pool, was located in this site. Apparently this was the emergency water supply for the fire tenders.

A short distance north of the Communal Site, on the left-hand side of the minor road, was another hutted site, labelled WAAF SITE, which contained quarters for the Women's Auxiliary Air Force personnel. On the right-hand side of this minor road was the site, labelled SITE No 2, described in the introduction. This was originally RAF quarters, but re-used as emergency civilian accommodation after the war.

A third domestic site, labelled SITE No 3, was situated on the right-hand side of the B1154 road to Brancaster, a few hundred metres north of the road junction, opposite a track leading off to Lugden Hill Farm. Site No 3 was also used as RAF sleeping quarters.

The farmhouse, Sunderland Farm, lies near the centre of the map. The original farmhouse, requisitioned at the beginning of the war, was used as aircrew sleeping quarters until it was bombed in 1941. The farmhouse was subsequently rebuilt in the same location.

Although not shown on the map, a galvanized water tower (Braithwaite tower) was situated on the opposite side of the road to the WAAF Site, near to the entrance of the track leading to the farmhouse. This water tower, with its associated pumping station, supplied water to all of the various RAF sites in the vicinity.

The rebuilt Sunderland Farmhouse in the early post-war period

A large hangar, which was near the farmhouse, is also missing from this map. The hangar was dismantled and removed several years ago. During the war, Docking also had several Blister hangars.

The airfield, containing grass runways, was located south east of Sunderland farmhouse. Although not clearly shown on the map, parts of the concrete perimeter track survive and are still in use as farm access roads. The location of the surviving control tower is near the centre of the map, at the bottom of the area labelled TECHNICAL SITE. Other surviving buildings, including one that originally served as the squadron flight office, a tractor store and an agricultural plant store, are still standing in the Technical Site. In addition, two air raid shelters and two brick and concrete gun posts (or pill boxes) still survive near the airfield.

Original aircraft hangar

7

The Docking to Burnham Market road and a railway line ran past the southern edge of the airfield. The railway, part of the Heacham to Wells line that was axed in the early 1960s, crossed the road at a point near the airfield, due south of Sunderland farmhouse. The railway lines were taken up some years ago and little sign of them exists today. A bomb dump or store, which was created near the north-east perimeter of the airfield, has also disappeared.

Docking, or Sunderland, Airfield was created in 1939, when the land, farmhouse and other buildings were requisitioned from the farmer, Mr William H.C. Peacock, who then moved out to Manor House, Brancaster for the duration of the war. The airfield was initially used as a decoy site and a protective dispersal site for the nearby permanent base of Bircham Newton, which was part of No. 16 Group of RAF Coastal Command. At night it was used as a so-called Q-site, to simulate the flarepath lighting of a permanent operational station and lure enemy bombers away from Bircham Newton and other potential targets in the area. During daylight hours it became a K-site, which was a decoy site designed to replicate the layout of an operational station, complete with dummy aircraft and other structures designed to fool the enemy. It was apparently very successful in this role, since it was bombed several times during this period without loss of human life. Docking was not the only decoy site used by Bircham Newton during the war. A dummy airfield was also maintained at Coxford Heath, near the village of Coxford, to divert enemy bombers away from Bircham and Sculthorpe, another operational base in the immediate area. A decoy site was also maintained near the village of Sedgeford, to the west of Docking. Even after it became operational in 1940, Docking was still used in this decoy role. As late as 1941, dummy Hurricane fighters were being placed around the airfield to fool the enemy into thinking that the area was well defended.

It wasn't long before Docking was being used as an emergency landing ground and satellite for Bircham Newton. Many of Bircham's aircraft were dispersed either temporarily or permanently to Docking and flew from its airstrip. Consequently, most of the Coastal Command operations that were undertaken by Bircham Newton also took place at Docking. However, most of the night flying was conducted at Docking, since the airfield was larger and flatter than Bircham Newton's airstrip and was equipped with better lighting than was available at the parent station.

Owing to the difficulty of landing at Bircham at night, and also to avoid attracting the attention of any German aircraft in the vicinity to the main base, all aircraft that arrived back during the hours of darkness landed at Docking, and were ferried back to Bircham, if necessary, at first light the next morning. Similarly, if there was the possibility of night operations, pilots were required each evening to ferry Bircham aircraft to Docking and to bring them back the following morning. One Canadian squadron coined a new name, 'The Docking Ferry', for the pilots who had to sacrifice those last few minutes of their beauty

8

sleep to ferry aircraft back from Docking. For operations during light evenings, it was possible for the aircraft to leave from Bircham but land at Docking on their return. There was a large interchange of aircraft between the two airfields throughout the war, although most of the aircraft maintenance and support continued from Bircham, which had facilities appropriate to a permanent pre-war RAF station.

Although it started life as Bircham Newton's satellite, Docking soon expanded and took on a life of its own. As the war progressed many visiting squadrons arrived from other RAF and naval stations, using Docking as a forward base to conduct anti-shipping and other offensive operations over the North Sea. The visitors included one Dutch, one Polish and two Canadian squadrons, which used the base for offensive operations off the Dutch coast. During its early operational life Docking, or Sunderland, airfield even had its own decoy site near the tiny hamlet of Egmere, but this was later developed into an operational airfield called RAF North Creake.

Some Public Records Office (AIR 10) data on Docking airfield as of December 1944 are provided below:

Grass Landing Area:

Directions	Dimensions
N.E. – S.W.	1730 yds, extendable to 4000 yds
E. – W.	1,400 yds, extendable to 2500 yds
N. – S.	1,100 yds, extendable to 2000 yds

Facilities:

Airfield Lighting	Mark II (Drem, Drem modified, 2 flare paths only)
Beam Approach	SBA
Radio	QDM
Flying Control	

Technical Accommodation:

Blister Hangars	Qty 8
A1 Hangar	Qty 1
No hard standings.	Dispersal is on grass within aerodrome boundary
Radio Facilities	HF/DF. 'Darky.' watch with frequencies 24 hours
Petrol Storage	144,000 galls aviation
Bomb Storage	18 tons

Domestic Accommodation

	Officers	SNCOs	ORs	Total
RAF	60	115	614	789
WAAF	2	2	88	92

This data indicates that the airfield accommodated a significant number of servicemen and women, not including those that were billeted in the surrounding villages and farms. Although the airfield possessed grass runways without aircraft hard standings, concrete perimeter tracks were provided. The airfield also possessed its own petrol storage facilities, a bomb dump and technical accommodation, including one permanent hangar and several blister hangars. Crew accommodation was provided in the requisitioned farmhouse, various hutments and several farm cottages. Batteries of Bofors anti-aircraft guns provided airfield defence.

Docking had a full range of flying control and landing aids. It possessed Drem lighting, which was a system of outer markings and approach lights, and two flare paths that could be illuminated at night. It possessed a HF/DF station, which could detect radio signals from aircraft and calculate the direction, or line of bearing, of the aircraft from the airfield. Pilots of returning aircraft would communicate with a W/T operator in flying control, who would provide bearings to home the aircraft onto the airfield. Standard Beam Approach (SBA) was also available to provide audible signals to assist pilots to land when the weather was bad or the visibility was very poor. Docking also provided a 'Darky' radio channel that was used by pilots who were lost or otherwise in distress.

Many different types of aircraft were to grace the skies over Docking as the war progressed. At the beginning of the war, the obsolescent Avro Anson 'Faithful Annie' was the mainstay of Coastal Command. Some Ansons flew from Bircham Newton and would also have been seen at Docking. However, Ansons were soon supplemented or replaced by Lockheed Hudsons and other aircraft. The Lockheed Hudson was a very common sight over Docking. This versatile twin-engined American aircraft began service with Coastal Command in a reconnaissance role, but its duties were quickly extended to anti-submarine, anti-shipping, convoy escort, meteorological reconnaissance and air-sea rescue (ASR). In this latter role it often carried an airborne lifeboat to rescue airmen that had ditched in the sea, or were 'down in the drink', as the RAF would say. In the meteorological role, another Lockheed aircraft, the Ventura, later replaced some of the Hudsons.

Two biplanes, which looked as though they belonged to the First World War, flew from Docking. One very famous biplane often seen was the Gloster Gladiator, the RAF's last biplane. This aircraft became famous in 1940 for the valiant defence of Malta, using three aircraft called Faith, Hope and Charity. At Docking Gladiators were used very successfully for gathering local meteorological data in all weather conditions. In fact, when the visibility was very

10

poor, it was often the only aircraft type that would be seen in the air. They were regularly seen in the skies around Docking until October 1944.

In 1942, Fairey Swordfish biplanes, affectionately known as 'Stringbags', belonging to the Fleet Air Arm, also flew on offensive anti-shipping and mine-laying operations from Docking and Bircham Newton. The 'Stringbag' nickname came from its versatility at carrying a variety of loads and also from its maze of bracing wires belonging to a bygone age. Despite its apparent obsolescence, this naval aircraft served with distinction throughout the war, gaining notoriety for crippling the German battleship Bismarck. Apparently, the 'Stringbag' had such a slow speed, that it was difficult for much faster monoplane fighters to fly slow enough to hold it in their sights for long enough to shoot it down. Similarly, most ship gun-crews had major difficulty targeting this biplane, since their guns were calibrated for use against much faster aircraft. One of Docking's visiting pilots, from 811 Squadron, who subsequently wrote about his war experiences flying the 'Stringbag', declared that 'it seemed to have been left in the war by mistake'. Later, Bircham Newton became the home to No. 119 Squadron, which also flew Swordfish aircraft. This squadron also possessed Albacore biplanes, which were frequently seen over Docking.

Three twin-engined monoplanes that were regularly seen at Docking were all manufactured by the Bristol Aeroplane Company: the Blenheim, Beaufort and Beaufighter. The Blenheim, which was used as a light bomber, long-range fighter and reconnaissance aircraft, was seen as early as 1940, but it was soon replaced because it was too slow and vulnerable. The Beaufort, a development of the Blenheim, specially adapted for Coastal Command to carry torpedoes, was also a regular early visitor. The Beaufighter was probably the most famous of the three, possessing much more speed and firepower; it replaced Blenheims and Beauforts as a long-range fighter and torpedo bomber and was often seen after 1941.

For long-range offensive operations, some of Docking's visiting squadrons flew the Vickers Wellington, a version of the twin-engined bomber aircraft that was the mainstay of Bomber Command during the early part of the war. This aircraft had a geodetic construction designed by Barnes Wallis, in which the airframe was constructed as a metal network and covered with fabric. This construction allowed the aircraft to survive damage from enemy gunfire that would destroy other aircraft types. Because of the fabric covering it was often nicknamed the 'cloth bomber' but to its aircrew it was affectionately known as the 'Wimpey', after Popeye's friend J. Wellington Wimpey.

Other ex-bombers that were adapted for Coastal Command duties and appeared at Docking included the Armstrong Whitworth Whitley, the Handley Page Hampden and the Vickers Warwick. Some of these aircraft carried micro-wave air-to-surface vessel (ASV) radar to detect enemy ships and submarines. The Warwick, unsuccessful in offensive operations, was adapted for air-sea rescue (ASR).

11

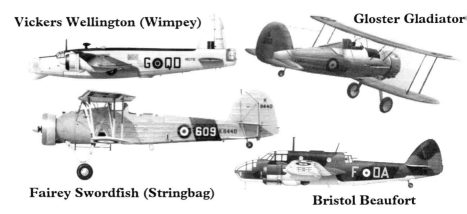

Vickers Wellington (Wimpey)

Gloster Gladiator

Fairey Swordfish (Stringbag)

Bristol Beaufort

By the late summer of 1942, a famous fighter-bomber and reconnaissance aircraft, the De Havilland Mosquito, known as the 'Mossie', appeared on the scene. The versatile 'Mossie' gained a fearsome reputation as a day and night fighter, anti-shipping attack and reconnaissance aircraft, despite the fact that it was primarily made of plywood and balsa. At Bircham Newton it was used in a weather reconnaissance role, conducting some night operations from Docking. Many other aircraft types visited or were based at Docking as the war progressed and these will be introduced later.

Squadron records indicate that initial operations from Docking were conducted in 1940 by Beaufort aircraft of 22 Squadron, Blenheim aircraft of 235 Squadron and Hudson aircraft of 206 Squadron.

Perhaps Docking's greatest individual contribution to the war effort was in the field of meteorological reconnaissance, which it took over from Bircham Newton in 1943. Number 1401 (Met) Flight, which later became 521 Squadron, flew meteorological operations from Docking using a variety of aircraft. This provided vital met data required for RAF bombing missions, to prevent aircraft from getting lost on their way to targets because of dense cloud or fog or changing wind conditions. Accurate met data also provided forecasts of expected weather conditions at home or dispersal bases for returning aircraft. By the nature of the task, met squadrons frequently flew in bad weather. Long periods of blind flying, coping with severe icing conditions, descents through heavy cloud and near-blind landings were the norm. Met flights were truly 'up in all weather' and were often of long duration, causing great discomfort and fatigue for the aircrew.

Many air-sea rescue (ASR) operations were also conducted from Docking, using Hudson aircraft of 279 Squadron, which were dispersed from Bircham Newton to use Docking during the hours of darkness. This squadron was used to locate ditched aircrew and rescue them by dropping dinghies or airborne lifeboats into the sea. From mid-1940 Docking was used continuously in these meteorological reconnaissance, air-sea rescue and anti-shipping/anti-submarine roles.

Since Docking is situated so close to the coast it was also frequently used as an emergency landing strip for aircraft returning damaged, lost or short of fuel from operational sorties. Many aircraft crashes associated with such forced landings occurred throughout the war.

Docking was home to a Beam Approach Training (BAT) flight, whose role was to train pilots in the use of a WW2 navigation aid installed on most large stations. It also hosted an armament practice camp (APC) flight, whose aircraft towed target drogues used for aircrew gunnery practice. Docking also briefly housed a Warwick Training Unit, used to prepare aircrew to fly the Warwick aircraft, which was being introduced into the ASR role.

Many operations, including meteorological reconnaissance, had moved from Docking to Langham, another satellite of Bircham Newton, by October 1944. However, some flying tasks continued into the summer of 1945. Coastal Command relinquished use of the station in late 1945, and it was finally sold off, surplus to requirements, in 1958. The land has now been returned to agricultural use. Sadly, little remains to identify Docking airfield today. Its lasting memorial is a dilapidated control tower, some perimeter track and a few other buildings converted for agricultural use.

The following squadrons were involved in official RAF movements to RAF Docking in WW2. Many used Docking as a forward base to conduct operations across the North Sea: 53, 143, 221, 235, 241, 254, 268, 288, 304, 407, 415, 502, 521, and 524

Other RAF squadrons were dispersed to Docking from Bircham Newton or flew from Docking at night to fulfil Bircham Newton's commitments. Some Fleet Air Arm Squadrons also made Docking their temporary home.

The control tower (watch office) and BAT flight office are shown right of centre in this early post-war photograph of the Technical Site

2. Meteorological Reconnaissance

'The sorties could be uneventful; and routine but uncomfortable in bad weather and sometimes extremely cold, especially when the heaters broke down.'

One of Docking's greatest contributions to the war effort was that of meteorological reconnaissance. Detailed knowledge of the weather was essential for conducting successful RAF operations in WW2. In particular, knowledge of the weather as it related to landing conditions for returning bombers was imperative. The most common questions would relate to the weather conditions at the home base for returning aircraft or requests for suitable alternative bases with favourable weather conditions. Information on wind speed, cloud formation, relative humidity and barometric pressure would be required to allow meteorological officers to create weather maps and make forecasts and recommendations about the feasibility of flying operations. To gather this data, long-range aerial reconnaissance was required. Initially navigators did weather observation on RAF flights, but it was decided to create a specialist Meteorological Observer in 1942. By the end of the war, 20 RAF Officers and 80 NCOs had been trained to perform this task.

One of the most important instruments consulted by a Met. Observer was a barometer, used for measuring atmospheric pressure. He would also consult a psychrometer, which measured the water vapour content or relative humidity of the atmosphere. A psychrometer contains two thermometers, called the 'dry bulb' and the 'wet bulb'. The latter is so called because a muslin cloth soaked in water surrounds its bulb. The 'wet bulb' temperature reading is usually lower than the 'dry bulb' reading, because of the cooling effect of the evaporation that occurs around the wet bulb. From these reading differences the Met. Observer could obtain a measure of the relative humidity of the atmosphere. A third instrument that was important to him was the air speed indicator, which would be used to make corrections to temperature readings due to the effect of air friction. The observer would also study and record the prevailing conditions, such as visibility, cloud cover, wind speed and the state of the sea that he was overflying.

In 1940 Coastal Command authorized the formation of three new flights for the purpose of gathering meteorological data. Number 403 Flight was formed at Bircham Newton. Subsequently, the flights were numbered in the 14-series, and 403 Flight became 1403 Flight, equipped with Blenheim Mk IV aircraft. In March 1941 Coastal Command was given overall responsibility for all meteorological units then operating throughout the RAF. As a result, the met flights were upgraded and renumbered. One of these, 1401 (Met) Flight, was established at Bircham Newton in February 1942 by absorbing 1403 Flight and the existing 1401 Flight with its Gladiator aircraft that had been based at Mildenhall in Suffolk. Many of the 1401 (Met) Flight operations were subsequently flown

14

from Docking. A variety of aircraft were used as part of the mixed equipment of this flight in addition to their original Blenheim IV and Gladiator aircraft. These included Hurricane, Hudson, Ventura and a pair of Spitfire F aircraft. The Spitfires were subsequently replaced with the more suitable Mosquito Mk IV for operational reconnaissance sorties over enemy territory.

Lockheed Hudson aircraft of the type flown by No. 521 Squadron

In August 1942, 1401 (Met) Flight was disbanded and reformed as 521 Squadron, with additional Spitfire Mk V aircraft for high altitude reconnaissance sorties. Confusingly, in March 1943, the squadron was subsequently disbanded and became 1401 Flight again, losing its Mosquito element, which moved to Oakington. No 521 Squadron was reformed at Docking in its previous role in September 1943. It was now equipped with Hampdens, Hudsons, and Gladiators. Hurricanes supplemented the Gladiators in August 1944.

Several of the Docking Gladiators were damaged or destroyed in local crashes in 1943 and 1944. One overturned after forced landing in semi darkness and poor visibility near King's Lynn in November 1943 after failing to find the aerodrome. Another hit a tree and overturned attempting to force-land in darkness after the engine cut out over sea near Boston, Lincolnshire in December 1943. Subsequent to this initial engine trouble, when the aircraft was still at 18,000 feet, the propeller and reduction gear detached themselves from the aircraft and the pilot, Sgt McKay, attempted to crash land in a field at Old Leake in Lincolnshire. The pilot was unhurt, but the aircraft was completely written off. A third aircraft swung off the runway at Great Massingham in March 1944 and hit an obstruction and a fourth hit a mast in fog at Docking in September 1944. Both were destroyed beyond repair.

No. 521 Squadron was organized into two flights, lettered R and T, which were abbreviations for meteorological codes RHOMBUS and THUM respectively. The Gladiators and their replacement Hurricanes performed Thermal Upper-Air Measurement (THUM) missions, which obtained temperature and humidity readings at various altitudes up to 30,000 ft. In performing THUM sorties, the aircraft would fly in spirals or on short reciprocal tracks, keeping within a few miles of the take-off airfield at Docking or Bircham.

Spitfires performed Pressure and Temperature Ascent (PRATA) missions. These were high altitude missions flown within ten miles of the airfield. The aircraft would first climb to 40,000 feet taking pressure and temperature readings every 5,000 feet. These missions were considered very onerous because they were of very long duration and required great precision in flying. The pilot had to level out at each standard height and maintain his altitude for two minutes to allow the instrument to settle down before being read. Visual observations such as cloud bases, formation of icing and condensation trails were also made. RHOMBUS was a code name given to reconnaissance flights that were performed on set tracks over the North Sea.

The long-range Rhombus sorties were carried out in twin-engined aircraft, initially Hampdens but later replaced by Hudsons and Venturas. The crew would consist of a pilot, navigator/met observer and two wireless operator/air gunners. One WOp/AG would be at the wireless set and the other in the gun turret. The first leg of the sortie would normally take place at low-level, making observations (barometric pressure, humidity, temperature, sea state, etc) every 50 nautical miles, descending to sea level for every third set of readings. At the end of the low-level leg, a 'boxed' ascent to 20,000 feet would be made, recording data at every drop of 50 millibars in air pressure. The aircraft would be levelled out at each of these 50-millibar increments to allow the readings to be taken. The final leg of the sortie consisted of a gradual descent back to base. During this return leg, the readings would be put into coded groups, which would be transmitted to a central headquarters by one of the WOp/AGs. During the sortie the crew would also report on the position of any enemy shipping and/or submarines sighted. These daily flights took off regardless of the weather.

On 10 October 1943, take-off for a Rhombus sortie was delayed owing to bad visibility and when an attempt was made, the Hampden aircraft crashed and was burned out when it swung on take-off and hit a gun post. Three members of

No. 521 Squadron enjoying the snow between operations

16

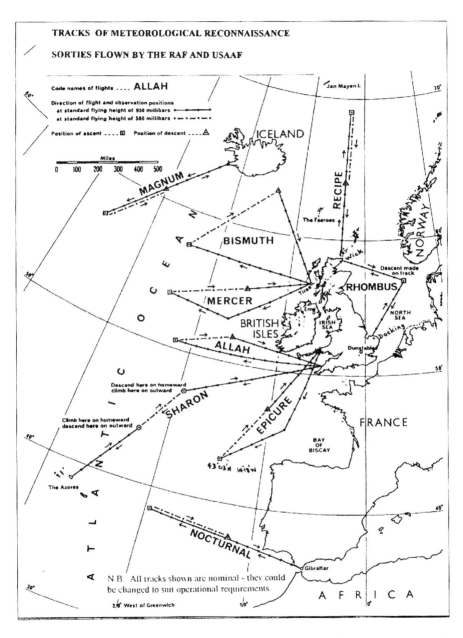

Tracks of wartime Meteriological Reconnaissance sorties with Rhombus tracks between Docking and Wick in Scotland

17

the crew were killed and the pilot and navigator were seriously injured in this unfortunate incident. The damaged gun post is thought to be standing on the derelict airfield today.

The 521 Squadron Operations Record Book succinctly describes the crash as follows:

10.10.43	Hampden 4204	Rhombus	Up 09.25
	Crashed taking off in low visibility		

F/O J. Maxwell
P/O W.D. Cooper
Sgt C. Curd
Sgt J. Allaway

The surviving navigator, Jack Allaway, explained that he managed to escape from the burning wreck when he saw daylight through a hole in the fuselage below him. Despite his burns, and the cramped conditions inside the Hampden, he was able to scramble out through this hole on the underside of the aircraft and make his escape. He thought that the aircraft must have come to rest over a ditch, providing sufficient space underneath the aircraft for him to get away. Jack said that he would never forget the screams of his colleagues who perished in the fire. Fortunately, his skipper and best friend, a Canadian named Jack Maxwell, managed to escape through the top of the aircraft. Jack Allaway was taken to the station sick quarters suffering from severe burns to his hands and face. He was quickly sent to the burns ward at the RAF hospital in Ely, where he was treated by one of the RAF's specialists in burns treatment, Wing Commander George Morley. He was later transferred to the Queen Victoria Hospital in East Grinstead, where he stayed for more than three years undergoing pioneering burns treatment and plastic surgery under the supervision of the senior plastic surgeon Archibald McIndoe. He was not declared fit to leave this hospital until 1947. McIndoe's 'army' of burns victims later formed the Guinea Pig Club, which is still going strong today, with Jack as one of its most active representatives.

521 Squadron was equipped with Ventura GR V aircraft in December 1943. In the same month, the Hampdens were declared operationally unserviceable and delivered to an aircraft factory for dismantling. The first operational Rhombus sortie in a Ventura, carried out on 5 December 1943, had to be abandoned after the aircraft suffered damage from machine-gun fire from an enemy vessel. This happened when the Ventura flew over the vessel to take photographs. The aircraft was hit in several places, including the camera, which was in the navigator's hand at the time. Luckily, no casualties were sustained. One of the Venturas crashed south of the airfield on 16 July 1945 after engine trouble. The pilot was unable to clear a clump of trees ahead and decided to

crash land. Before coming to a halt, the aircraft went through a hedge and caught fire. The crew and passengers (two air cadets) escaped with slight cuts and burns, but the aircraft sustained irreparable damage.

A Rhombus sortie involved flying diagonally out across the North Sea from Docking to a point just south of Norway and then back towards Wick in Scotland, returning on the following day. These sorties lasted for four to five hours, depending on the wind speed and direction. One flight was generally conducted in daylight hours and the other at night. A sister squadron, 519 Squadron, performed a similar operation, taking off from its home base at Skitten near Wick and flying the rhombus in the reverse direction to Docking. Consequently, the crews of the two squadrons became well acquainted with each other through their contact in the messes. 519 Squadron Venturas were a common site at Docking. These flights were known as the Shuttle Rhombus sorties. Data gathered during Rhombus sorties was encoded using a specially-devised five-figure code, which was then transmitted to Group Headquarters.

This is a typical Shuttle Rhombus schedule conducted on 2 October 1944

> Hudson P/519   airborne Skitten 0357
> landed Docking 0800
>
> Hudson M/521   airborne Docking 1000
> landed Skitten 1457

In *Even the Birds were Walking*, a navigator with 521 Squadron, J. H. Seymour, part of an all-Australian crew, recalls Rhombus sorties between Docking and Wick in Hudson and Ventura aircraft. His first operational sortie with 521 Squadron, in April 1944, involved a flight to Wick departing from Docking at 1200 hrs. The flight, in a Ventura aircraft, which lasted for 4 hours 40 minutes, was via Norwegian fiords. The next morning at 0600 hrs his aircraft departed from Wick to fly back to Docking, again via the Norwegian fiords. He recalled that they flew at varying altitudes between 50 ft and 20,000 ft above sea level. They had to maintain their different heights for an interval of time while they gathered the required met data. This Australian crew completed 38 sorties in Ventura aircraft before the squadron reverted to Hudson and later Fortress aircraft.

This account given by a pilot from 519 Squadron, Warrant Officer Les Hart, reproduced with his kind permission, gives a good impression of what a Rhombus sortie was like.

'Our job was gathering meteorological information. 519 squadron flew two met flights, one code named Recipe, from Wick, more or less due north over Arctic waters, at 1200 to 1500 feet to a sea position some 500 miles away (750 miles in the case of the Fortress), taking readings from special instruments of barometric pressure, temperatures, humidity, cloud formations, sea state, etc, every 50 nautical miles, and descending to sea level every 150 nautical miles for further readings. At the sea position extremity of the flight, a box climb was made to approximately 18-20,000 feet in the Ventura, and 25-30,000 feet in the Fortress, levelling out at regular 50-millibar intervals to take further readings. The information was recorded on special forms and then converted into a five-figure code with a Syko machine. At the top of the climb and with all data coded, the aircraft set course in a gradual descent back to base, the wireless operators taking turns to transmit the data back to Group Headquarters. No further readings were taken, but all crew not otherwise engaged searched for enemy U-boats. Depth charges were carried should an attack be mounted. The Recipe sortie averaged some 7 to 8 hours flying time in the Ventura and Hudson, and from 10 to 14 hours in the Fortress.

519 squadron also flew the Rhombus sortie which tracked from Wick across the North Sea to a sea position off the Skaggerack, where a similar climb was made, followed by a gradual descent to an airfield called Docking (later at Langham) in Norfolk, where after a debriefing, the crew had a meal, got some sleep and performed the identical trip in reverse back to Wick the next day. For both the Recipe and Rhombus, two sorties were flown each 24 hours, one day and one night.

The sorties could be uneventful and routine but uncomfortable in bad weather and sometimes extremely cold, especially when the heaters broke down. For this reason we wore silk and wool long sleeved vests and long johns, a thick woollen sweater and socks, battledress and sheepskin lined leather Irvin jackets and trousers. But with all that you could get chilled to the bone, happily not on every trip.

All this became necessary because at the outbreak of war the Met Service was deprived of all the reports on weather transmitted to them by ships plying across the Atlantic and around the coasts of Britain, and the special weather ships that had been anchored in the oceans. If they had continued to transmit, enemy submarines would have been able to locate and destroy them.

The dangers facing us were insidious and arose from the weather. Icing in the carburettors and building up on the wings were a hazard. Flying low over the wave tops at night to obtain sea level readings when rough weather made it extremely bumpy and visibility was nil, was also difficult. And to arrive home after a long and tiring trip to discover fog or a very low cloud base over the airfield made landing a prolonged and difficult task. Sometimes in such conditions we were diverted to other airfields such as Stornoway or Tain, but there were occasions when fuel was too low to do so and risks had to be taken to get down on the ground.'

Warrant Officer pilot Les Hart (standing centre) with his 521 Squadron Fortress crew in 1945.

No. 521 Squadron also flew the so-called PAMPA flights over occupied Europe in all weathers to obtain meteorological data relating to target areas. Most of the flights involved deep penetration into enemy territory to determine the expected weather for that night's heavy bomber raid, especially over the target area. These were initially conducted by 521 Squadron Spitfires but were suspended when four aircraft failed to return. PAMPA flights were resumed after 521 Squadron received Mosquito aircraft in 1942. The Mosquito was one of the most versatile aircraft of the Second World War. It was constructed of wood and had an exceptionally streamlined design; with its two-man crew and greater endurance it proved ideal for 521 Squadron's PAMPA operations. The first Mosquito PAMPA sortie was conducted at Bircham Newton on 2 July 1942. PAMPA aircraft were generally placed on standby ready to take off in any weather to gather data over the target area ahead of a planned bomber raid. The Mosquito proved so successful in this role that it remained as the standard PAMPA aircraft until the end of the war. The eight Mosquitos of 521 Squadron were transferred to Oakington in April 1943 to become part of 1409 Flight.

In their book *Even the Birds were Walking* John Kingdom & Peter Ratcliff document two Mosquito PAMPA flights over occupied territory in 1942 made by W.J. 'Bill' Davis, a WOp/AG and Navigator of 521 Squadron. Bill, who now lives at Happisburgh in Norfolk, joined 521 Squadron in December 1941. This short extract from his diary entry for 4 September 1942 vividly describes the excitement and danger of such a PAMPA flight.

21

'Squadron Leader Braithwaite was my pilot and the trip was Bremen and Hamburg. We took off at 5 PM, crossed the Dutch coast at 28,000 feet in clear sky and were met by two Focke Wulf 190s over the Zuyder Zee. What a fight we had, it lasted 30 minutes – 30 minutes of hell. Thank God we out turned and out flew them, only getting one bullet hole. I felt done in after the terrible throwing around we endured. Wing tip was also shot away.'

The next day, in his diary, Bill complained of feeling physically and mentally sick, with every bone in his body aching and his nerves shot to bits. He said it would be a long time before he forgot seeing cannon shells coming towards him. Squadron Leader Braithwaite, who was his CO, thanked Bill for the way he kept cool during the incident, giving him good instructions throughout.

Although he was stationed and billeted at Bircham Newton, Bill was able to recall many flights from Docking. In conversation with the author, he said that the Squadron initially had Blenheims, which were far too slow and vulnerable to enemy fighters. Later in his time they were re-equipped with Hudsons, but these too were very vulnerable against enemy aircraft. He sadly recalled that he lost many friends who were shot down over the sea. Bill left the squadron in March 1943 to begin service in the Far East. Bill Davis returned to Docking in September 1944 as the CO of No. 2 Armament Practice Camp. In addition to target-towing aircraft, Bill was also responsible for some target-towing launches that were based at Wells-next-the-Sea. After VE-day he became CO of Docking and was responsible for closing down the operational side of the base in 1946, which was the year that he was discharged.

Bill Davis in front of a 521 Squadron Blenheim Mk IV aircraft

3. Air-Sea Rescue

'Something in the subconscious made me grab the emergency pump handle, which was connected between a small fuel tank and the carburettor, and the engines spluttered back into life.'

Although RAF bombers were equipped with dinghies, fighter pilots only had their Mae West life jackets. It was not until 1941 that fighter pilots began to be equipped with dinghy packs attached to their parachute harnesses. Consequently, early in the war it was realized that airmen who had to ditch in the sea needed immediate assistance, particularly the unfortunate fighter pilots. Various rescue packs were developed for dropping from aircraft, and eventually the 'Lindholme Gear' evolved, consisting of an inflatable dinghy plus several supply packs, linked together by floating rope. The supply packs contained food, water, first-aid kits and waterproof sleeping suits. The rescue aircraft that located ditched aircrew would drop the rescue

pack and fix the position of the survivors so that they could be located by one of the RAF's rescue launches or by Royal Navy or coastguard vessels.

At the end of November 1941 No. 279 Air Sea Rescue (ASR) Squadron was formed at Bircham Newton and No. 280 ASR Squadron was formed at Thorney Island. No. 279 Squadron, operational by March 1942, was equipped with Lockheed Hudson aircraft and No 280 Squadron, which became operational in June of the same year, was initially given Avro Anson aircraft. These two squadrons could carry out deep search operations and provide assistance to ditched aircrew by dropping Lindholme Gear.

Although air-sea rescue was Bircham Newton's task, many ASR operations were flown from Docking, particularly those that were conducted in the hours of darkness. A typical night operation from Docking, conducted on 4 May 1942, illustrates the difficulty of locating and rescuing ditched aircrew at night.

Aircraft V-Victor (V/279) took off from Docking at 0433 hours to carry out a search for a ditched Wellington, returning back to base at 0924 hours. The following extract, is taken from an entry in the Operations Record Book:

'V/279 took off from Docking to carry out a Sea Rescue Night Patrol. A last fix had previously been received from a Wellington a/c in distress at coordinate MBGM 2554. At 0516 this position was reached and flame floats were dropped it being too dark to search. After circling the position for six minutes, a course was set for coordinate MBBR 5443, being the previous fix of the Wellington a/c, with intention of flying up and down that track until broad daylight. Two white flashing lights sighted at 0524 but no more recognizable. After circling for four minutes, it was concluded that the flashes were caused by the flame floats dying out. Then decided to resume original track. At 0528 hours turret gunner saw a Signal Distress Marine two miles dead astern, and informed pilot who altered course by 180 degrees. A flare float was dropped after 1 minute the S.D.M having ceased. At 0530 hours a second S.D.M was observed about miles from float. Flew over S.D.M and sighted dinghy in its glow. Dropped additional flame floats and made sighting reports. Lost sight of dinghy at 0609 hours from a height of 2000 feet. Sighted Wellington a/c floating with tail fin above water. Set course downwind and resighted dinghy at 0613 hours. Five or six occupants could be seen in dinghy, four of whom stood up and expressed great joy. Dropped Lindholme dinghy and Wellington Dinghy eventually drifted within reach of it. U/279 and A/279 arrived at 0715. Rescue carried out by two MLS at 0839 hours.'

Another report of this V/279 sortie, made by the observer, mentions also that they sighted a Ju88 and took avoiding action. 279 Squadron crews often encountered enemy aircraft during search and rescue operations, as the following two incidents illustrate. On 2 June 1942, several aircraft were on a search and sighted a dinghy with four men on board. They had been attracted by smoke and coloured pyrotechnics. One of the aircraft dropped a Lindholme dinghy, which failed to open. This aircraft, Hudson P/279, was then attacked by two Me 109s. The pilot took evasive action, but the Hudson was hit and the observer and rear gunner were wounded. However, the crew believed that they had shot one of the enemy aircraft down. The pilot managed to land safely at Eastchurch with over 100 holes in the fuselage. At 0200 hrs on 19 April 1944, Hudson L/279 was dispatched from Docking to cover the tracks of returning American bombers. During this sortie nothing was sighted except for numerous white lights on the water, which were presumed to be fishing vessels. On returning from the sortie the Hudson pilot turned downwind in the Docking circuit with his landing lights on. He observed the exhaust trails of an aircraft overhead, but this was disregarded when he was given the green light to land. Having landed and turned off the runway, he switched off his landing lights. He instantly heard three bursts of cannon fire from the starboard beam, although no hits were received. He quickly extinguished all lights and switched off the engines. Then to his great

24

surprise he observed an enemy aircraft (believed to be a Me 410) pulling out of a steep dive only about 30 feet from the ground.

Frank Goff in 1941

One ex-RAF pilot, Flight Lieutenant Frank Goff, had two tours of duty at Bircham Newton during WW2. Following his initial flying training in 1940, and conversion training on the Hudson aircraft in early 1941, Frank was posted to Bircham to join 206 Squadron. He recalled that his night-flying training was conducted after joining the Squadron, using the satellite airfield at Langham. After a short period at Bircham Newton, he accompanied part of the Squadron on a move to Gambia in West Africa, where they were renumbered as 200 Squadron. On the first leg of his journey to Africa, Frank flew his Hudson from Docking to Gibraltar, a flight of approximately 11 hours duration. After a short break in Gibraltar, he flew as navigator on the second leg of the journey from Gibraltar to Bathurst, which lasted for more than 13 hours! In late 1943, following his return to UK and a tour as part of No. 6 Operational Training Unit at RAF Silloth, Frank returned to Bircham Newton to join 279 Squadron on air sea rescue duties. His second tour at Bircham was to last one year, including most of 1944.

Frank explained that Bircham's grass runway was really too short for night take-offs and not very level. Consequently, during his time at Bircham Newton, 279 Squadron usually had one or more aircraft on night stand-by at Docking. He recalled the last operational night flight – a very short one - made by 279 Squadron from Bircham Newton airfield.

'It was in early 1944 and I was the Squadron Duty Officer. The standby night aircraft was a MK IV Hudson with Pratt & Whitney engines. This mark of the Hudson was not so lively as the aircraft fitted with Cyclone engines, and required a greater length of runway for take off. The night in question was slightly misty and dead calm. The flare path had been set for the longest run, as there was no wind and it was an uphill takeoff. There was a call at 9:30 PM and I had to get the crew from the camp cinema. I remember that the skipper, P/O Curtis, was not very happy about the aircraft, but it was serviceable and I told him to use a bit of flap to help her off. I watched them start off across the grass runway but the aircraft never really got off the ground. They lifted the undercarriage at the far edge of the airfield and disappeared into the scrub. The aircraft was well loaded with flares, and we had a terrific firework display when they went up. Fortunately, the crew scrambled out before the aircraft burned. After this incident, Bircham's airfield was not used any more for night operations. We always flew to Docking with two aircraft for night standby.'

Frank remembered that when on night standby at Docking they used a cottage at the edge of the airfield that was equipped with several beds. He recalled one occasion when his crew had been placed on night standby at very short notice. The trouble was that his navigator, F/O Cook, had disappeared to Brancaster for the evening, to have a drink in one of his favourite pubs. Frank decided to fly the navigator's gear over to Docking in the hope of finding him. Fortunately Frank was later able to contact the pub landlord by telephone with urgent instructions for Cook to report to Docking as soon as possible. The embarrassed navigator duly appeared and the panic was over. Luckily there had been no call-out in the period that he was absent, since it would have been impossible to conduct a night search over the North Sea without a navigator. The navigator's position was down in the nose of the Hudson, reached by descending steps positioned near where a second pilot would be seated in other aircraft. However, Frank's navigator, F/O Cook, was nervous about working in the nose of the aircraft, some distance away from the escape exit above the cockpit. Consequently, he used to sit on the steps, using part of a NAAFI tea chest as his chart table. He would navigate using the cockpit instruments, assessing wind speed and direction by observing the 'wind lanes' on the surface of the sea. Frank recalled one flight when they had a high-ranking American on board. The American was sitting on the steps, forcing F/O Cook to occupy the conventional navigator's position down in the nose of the aircraft. Everything was fine until one of the engines cut out. In a great panic, Cook rushed up the steps, with his personal life vest in hand, trampling all over the surprised American. A few seconds later, the engine re-started and the embarrassed Cook had to descend the dreaded steps again, back to his cramped position below. Frank understood his navigator's desire to be near an escape hatch. The Hudson could easily burn. The fuel tanks were inside the wings and the undercarriage could be pushed up into the fuel tanks as a result of a crash or even a very heavy landing. This would release fuel, which would easily ignite from any stray sparks. Also, the Hudson quickly sank if it was ditched in the sea.

Frank said that night searches could be full of surprises, and he illustrated it with the following example.

'We were on night standby at Docking one night when we were called out for a search. There was no Moon, it was cloudy and a very dark night. A Mosquito intruder aircraft had developed engine trouble returning from Germany and when the aircraft was about a mile off Bacton the pilot told the navigator to bale out as he was going to ditch. However, the pilot just made it to the beach and put the aircraft down on the sand. He reported the position and we flew down and started searching. The night aircraft was loaded with parachute flares, which

26

the WOp/AGs pushed out through the retractable belly door. This was the original luggage-loading door in the civilian version of the Hudson – the Lockheed 14 airliner. We flew at about 700 feet, and as soon as the flares ignited we circled around looking at the surface of the sea. Of course, after a few minutes of tightish left-hand turns gradually getting lower, the compass and gyro instruments went off balance and spun. This had just occurred when we had a complete engine failure. Something in the subconscious made me grab the emergency pump handle, which was connected between a small fuel tank and the carburettor, and the engines spluttered back into life. I switched to another main tank having realized that while concentrating on the search I had forgotten to change tanks. I was very glad that the crew could not see how close we were to going down in the drink. Unfortunately we did not locate the survivor before we ran out of flares and had to abort the search.'

Frank explained that coastal squadrons operating from Bircham Newton and Docking were often caught out by low cloud or North Sea haze drifting inland. Consequently, to get back to base, the pilots would fly at low-level round the coast to Hunstanton and fly in over the pier, pick up the Docking road and follow it to Docking airstrip. He said that he had only used this technique once, in November 1943, when returning from an air-sea rescue search. He picked up the Docking road, but half way to Docking the cloud had descended to tree-top height, so he did a sharp climbing U-turn, eventually spotting the beach at Brancaster. He then followed the coast round to Sutton Bridge, where there was a fighter airfield in the position that is now occupied by a power station. The fighter pilots didn't get many visitors, so they made Frank and his crew very welcome in their mess.

Air-sea rescue aircraft were often dispatched to patrol the route of returning bombers. This involved lengthy missions, involving multiple aircraft and crews. One example occurred on the afternoon of 22 February 1944, when two Hudsons of 279 Squadron were dispatched at 1530 hrs to patrol the tracks of returning USAAF bombers. Unfortunately, one of the aircraft had to return to base owing to engine trouble. However, the returning crew was quickly transferred to a replacement aircraft, taking off at 1613 hrs. At 1729 hrs the first of the Hudsons, E/279, sighted two American dinghies lashed together containing about ten airmen. The rescue aircraft reported the survivor's position and dropped them a Lindholme package, which overshot the American airmen and failed to open. E/279 then made contact with the second aircraft, J/279, piloted by Frank Goff, which successfully dropped a Lindholme package and witnessed the Americans reaching it in their dinghies. E/279 was then ordered to stay on station until relief arrived. While patrolling the area, Frank sighted smoke about 20 miles away and went to investigate. A large patch of oil was found, and an airman was seen nearby floating in the water attached to a parachute. A smoke float was dropped, but the airman and parachute disappeared below the surface. After further unsuccessful searches for other survivors, Frank returned to Docking, landing at 2000hrs. Meanwhile E/279 sighted the rescue launch, which it homed onto the survivors using its landing lights. It then returned to Docking, landing at 2145 hrs. A third aircraft, D/279 had been dispatched at 1846 hrs to relieve E/279, but by the time it arrived on the scene and made contact with E/279 the rescue was complete. So it returned to Docking, landing at 2201 hrs. This operation, which was fairly typical, had lasted approximately six and a half hours and had involved four aircraft and three crews.

Frank Goff remembered how pleased he was to reach Docking airstrip on 22 April 1944, whist he was ferrying the Air Officer Commanding, AVM Hopps, back from Detling in Kent to Bircham Newton late in the evening. Frank recalled that they followed the coastline, giving a wide berth to the Thames estuary and Felixstowe, to avoid the trigger-happy gun batteries usually encountered in those areas. It was quite dark as they turned inland over Aldeburgh at about 1,500 feet, well below the tracks of returning American bombers, who would be above them at about 10,000 feet. He realized that something unusual was happening when he spotted fires and explosions on the ground beneath them. Frank guessed that intruding enemy aircraft had shot down several returning bombers, as they were limping back to their home bases. His fears were confirmed when he spotted an enemy fighter (Me 410) a few hundred yards away on his port beam. The Germans were obviously confused to find a smaller twin-engined aircraft in the vicinity and did not fire. Presumably they were trying to identify Frank's aircraft or had confused his silhouette with that of a Dornier. Before his own air gunner could begin to fire at the intruder, Frank dropped down to 500 feet and made a dash for Docking, where he landed, safely and much relieved, a few minutes later. Frank later learned that the unfortunate American bombers, part of the infamous Mission 311, had been returning from an evening bombing raid on the German marshalling yard at Hamm. A large number of Fortress and Liberator aircraft were shot down over the target area, and enemy fighters downed many more as they limped back to their bases in East Anglia. Frank rarely encountered American bombers, since they flew at a much higher altitude. However, on more than one occasion, he had experienced a near miss with a falling Fortress propeller, descending like a sycamore seedpod from the sky above.

At about the time that 279 ASR Squadron was forming, consideration was being given to the design of a form of powered lifeboat that could be dropped by an aircraft. In January 1942 a contract was placed with the famous yachtsman Uffa Fox to build a fleet of airborne lifeboats. The Mark I version of the resulting lifeboat was initially built to be carried by 279 ASR Squadron Hudson aircraft, while the Mark IA was developed for the Hudson's successor, the Vickers Warwick aircraft. The initial batches of 27 ft airborne lifeboats, which could carry up to 16 survivors, were made of mahogany and fitted with twin outboard petrol engines. They also had a mainsail and a foresail plus four long oars. In addition to food, water, cigarettes and waterproof clothing, onboard survival equipment included a radio transmitter and receiver, a Very pistol with cartridges, a torch and an Aldis signal lamp. Sealed instruction booklets on sailing principles and engine starting procedures were also provided.

The lifeboat had to be released by the ASR aircraft at an altitude between 600 and 700 feet while flying into wind. Bombsights were used to judge accurately the precise moment for release. The lifeboat dropped to the sea suspended either on six small or three large parachutes. CO_2 bottles inflated two buoyancy chambers on the boat as it left the aircraft to ensure that it did not sink as it hit the water. In order to keep the lifeboat's head into wind, a sea anchor was fired during the descent. It was a very skilled operation that took some time and practice to perfect. The following examples illustrate some successful drops of airborne lifeboats and underscore some of the difficulties encountered by the rescued airmen.

In *Unsung Heroes of R.A.F. Air Sea Rescues* Stephen Brewster Daniels describes the first operational drop of an airborne lifeboat from a 279 ASR Squadron Hudson to a ditched Halifax crew from 102 Squadron in the North Sea. The lifeboat was dropped within 25 yards of the dinghy containing the aircrew, who were able to board it and set course for home. However this was the prelude to many problems, including the shearing of both lifeboat propellers and difficulties with the rigging and in raising the mainsail. However, despite the foggy conditions, searching planes later spotted the lifeboat and surface vessels were radioed to intercept it. The crew were subsequently picked up by one of the RAF's high-speed launches and landed at Grimsby.

In his book *Fly for their Lives,* John Chartres describes the first six operational airborne lifeboat drops. No. 279 ASR Squadron carried out some of these initial drops, as was illustrated by the first drop outlined above. Another 279 ASR Squadron success is illustrated by drop number six. This drop involved the rescue of the crew of a Mitchell aircraft of 226 Squadron, who ditched in July 1943. This Mitchell aircraft had been carrying out its own ASR operation when enemy fighters shot it down. A 279 ASR Squadron Hudson successfully dropped the survivors an airborne lifeboat, but things went terribly wrong after they got aboard. The lifeboat was swamped by large wind-driven waves and this stopped the engines. The survivors then tried to sail the lifeboat until the tiller arm broke. They spent two miserable days and nights in the lifeboat pumping and bailing out water as they drifted helplessly, but were eventually spotted by aircraft and picked up exhausted by Royal Navy rescue launches. They reached landfall a full three days after their aircraft had ditched.

The rescue launches and other surface craft were most important in air sea rescue operations. The Lindholme dinghies, and even the airborne lifeboats, were seen as a means of keeping the rescued airmen afloat and supplying them with food and water until rescue boats arrived on the scene. Coastal Command

A 279 ASR squadron Hudson carrying the airborne lifeboat

had marine craft units at Bridlington, Grimsby, Gorleston and Felixstowe, equipped with high-speed launches, to rescue ditched airmen from the perils of the North Sea. Similarly, the Royal Navy possessed rescue motor launches at Yarmouth, Lowestoft and Immingham on the Humber. In addition to these service rescue craft, lifeboat stations were situated all along the East coast, including those at Cromer, Sheringham and Wells-next-the Sea, quite close to Bircham Newton and Docking. The RAF rescue aircraft would attempt to coordinate the rescues by searching for the ditched aircrew, dropping them a Lindholme dinghy and then communicating with the rescue launches using the 500 KHz frequency reserved for distress calls. Having contacted a rescue boat the rescue aircraft was supposed to circle around the ditched airmen and continue to transmit continuously on this distress frequency to enable the launch to home onto it using its direction-finding aerial. Often the aircraft would also drop a flame float or something similar to mark the position of the aircrew dinghy. A companion aircraft, if available, would then fly over the launch, circle it and then fly back towards the ditched airmen, waggling its wings to provide the direction.

In his book *Air-Sea Rescue in World War Two*, Alan Rowe describes the combined rescue of the crew of a Lancaster bomber from the North Sea in September 1943. Four 279 ASR Squadron Hudsons from Docking and Bircham Newton were involved in this rescue. An initial two aircraft were sent from standby at Docking in the early morning to locate the downed aircraft and survivors in response to the distress call. They found the ditched Lancaster and the survivors nearby in a dinghy. One of the Hudsons dropped the Lindholme Gear, but the dinghy did not open and one of the containers burst. However, the ditched crew members were able to retrieve other containers, which contained rations. Two more 279 ASR Squadron Hudson aircraft were dispatched from Bircham Newton, one carrying an airborne lifeboat. This was successfully dropped into the sea and boarded by the five surviving Lancaster crew members, who then set off towards the English coast. Meanwhile one of the Hudsons circled continuously above them, sending out a signal on the distress frequency. To complete the rescue, a Royal Navy launch was guided by radio to the lifeboat by the Hudson aircraft. One aircraft guided the launch by radio, while the other

30

found the naval launch, circled it and then headed back towards the surviving aircrew, waggling its wings as a sign that naval launch should follow. The naval launch subsequently rescued the grateful airmen and landed them on shore. However, the naval crew failed to sink the Lancaster, which remained floating for several hours, despite attacks by guns and depth charges.

Another rescue mission undertaken by Frank Goff on 3 October 1944 was extracted from 279 Squadron's operational records:

'Flight Lieutenant Goff took off just after midday to seek one man in a dinghy off the Dutch coast, escorted by P-47 Thunderbolt fighters of the USAAF. Survivor found close to the Frisian Island of Schiermonnikoog. Hudson 'U' dropped lifeboat 100 yards down wind of him in a moderate westerly breeze. He was seen to board it and then flop down in the stern, utterly exhausted. Shadowed by the P-47s until darkness, he made no attempt to start the engines. Contact was lost after nightfall. It was hoped that it drifted ashore on the enemy coast. He could have been a survivor of B-17s. Two collided off this coast on the 30 September belonging to the 487th or 493rd Bomb Groups. It was reported by other combat crews that one Fortress fell due to battle damage, taking the second with it into the sea. If this airman was from one of the above aircraft, he had been in the water for 72 hours by the time of the lifeboat drop.'

On that occasion, Frank said, the lifeboat parachutes had failed to release on hitting the water. The survivor should have chopped the ropes through with the axe provided, but he remained motionless. Frank also confirmed that the survivor should have followed the message inside the lifeboat, instructing him to start up and head off in an easterly direction. They had buzzed him a few times to try and raise his interest, but they finally had to leave him as the fighters were getting low on fuel.

Mark I airborne lifeboat

31

ASR operations were dangerous operations that cost the lives of some rescue crews. In his book *Rescue from the Skies*, Stephen B. Daniels describes how one of 279 Squadron's Hudson aircraft was lost during a search for a dinghy from an aircraft, which had been shot down in the sea off Lowestoft. The unfortunate Hudson was seen by a neighbouring searcher to flip over before spiralling into the sea. Only one survivor, a Canadian, was subsequently rescued from the sea by a ship in the area. The ship also retrieved one dead body seen floating in a Mae West life jacket. Frank Goff, who was piloting one of the rescue aircraft on this particular rescue mission and was the sole witness at the subsequent enquiry, takes up the story.

'On 19 August 1944, which was a fine summer's day, 'Botha' Blake was piloting one of four aircraft searching for a ditched fighter pilot about a mile off Great Yarmouth. We had been searching for about 3 hours and were flying at about 500 feet and ¼ mile apart in a northerly direction. Blake was on my port side and nearest to the beach. In the few seconds that it took me to scan the sea to my right and the other aircraft, he had climbed to around 800 feet and was inverted and flying in the opposite direction. Naturally the Hudson did not take kindly to this manoeuvre, and I watched in horror as the nose dropped and she spiralled into the sea. Both motors appeared to be at normal revs. There was a large column of water spray and steam, and when this cleared there were only a few small pieces and some petrol on the surface. However, after a few seconds, a dinghy came up, having been automatically inflated. A few seconds later a body surfaced in a Mae West life jacket. He swam to the dinghy and hung on. Fortunately a minesweeper had been working less than ¼ mile away, and she steamed over and picked him up. The survivor was the WOp/AG, a Canadian, who owed his life to the fact that he had the night before been on a 'bender' in King's Lynn and was on that trip as the wireless operator. Just before the coast he had felt so rotten from his hangover that he changed with the gunner and had gone to the back turret to get some fresh air and have a smoke. He could not remember a thing, and we could only assume that the aircraft broke at the turret and some how he floated out as the aircraft sank. My wife went to see him several times in the Norfolk and Norwich Hospital, where they set his broken thigh and he slowly changed colour from black and blue to green and yellow. He was one enormous bruise'

No. 279 ASR Squadron was based at Bircham Newton from November 1941 until October 1944. It was initially equipped with Hudson III aircraft but was later upgraded to Hudson V and Hudson VI aircraft. During this time, aircraft were flown from Docking and detached to many other bases, including St Eval in Cornwall and Reykjavic in Iceland. Merv Hambling's book about

Norfolk air crashes (Bibliography 10) lists several 'prangs' by 279 ASR Squadron Hudson aircraft in 1942, 1943 and 1944. These include two crashes on forced landing at Docking. No. 279 ASR Squadron moved to Thornaby in Yorkshire in October 1944, where it was upgraded with Warwick and other aircraft. No. 280 ASR Squadron also had periods at Bircham and Docking with Anson I aircraft (1942) and Warwick I aircraft (1943).

The Lifeboat dropped by Frank Goff on 3 October, 1944

4. Offensive Operations

'The dawn scene at Docking must often have been very surprising to its resident airmen, with strange damaged aircraft scattered around the various dispersals.'

At the beginning of the war, during 1939 and early 1940, the duties of Coastal Command were confined to reconnaissance, convoy escort and submarine spotting, with an occasional attack on enemy ships. Top priority was given to protecting the North Sea fishing fleet ('kipper' patrols), protecting allied shipping convoys and mounting 'anti-invasion' patrols, looking for signs of the expected German invasion across the channel. Modern aircraft and other equipment were scarce. Moreover, the available aircraft were slow, under-armed and vulnerable to enemy aircraft. Consequently, early successes were minimal and losses in men and aircraft were very high. Attacks against enemy shipping were particularly costly, since the convoys were often escorted by fighter aircraft and included heavily armed flak ships. In these early days Coastal Command crews suffered appalling losses of up to 20 per cent on single sorties.

Gradually, the available aircraft were modernized, resulting in an expansion of duties for Coastal Command, which took on a more aggressive role. Although this modernization was under way during 1940 and 1941, many of the command's resources were diverted to other areas, such as the Mediterranean, where they were used to help cut Rommel's supply lines. Bomber Command and Fighter Command were also given preferential treatment in the allocation of aircraft and other resources. The modernization of Coastal Command was given fresh impetus by the 'Channel Dash' in February 1942. In this incident, the German warships *Scharnhorst, Gneisenau* and *Prinz Eugen* sailed from Brest to Germany in daylight and were virtually undamaged, despite the best efforts of the RAF and Royal Navy. To its acute embarrassment, Coastal Command was held to be primarily responsible for failing to locate and attack these warships. However, the Air Ministry later attributed this failure to a serious lack of resources.

The modernization of Coastal Command was slow, prior to 1942. Blenheim and Beaufort torpedo bombers were introduced to replace the ageing Vildebeest, which was the main torpedo bomber available at the beginning of the war. American-built Hudsons were put into service as fast as they could be procured to replace the ageing Ansons. Faster and better-armed Beaufighters were eventually introduced and adapted to carry out an anti-shipping role. Later, Wellington and other bomber aircraft were transferred from Bomber Command and adapted for flights of long duration over the sea. Some of these ex-bombers were fitted with microwave radar (ASV), to detect enemy surface vessels and submarines that were on the surface. Used in conjunction with the powerful Leigh searchlight, they were able to surprise the surface vessels and surfaced submarines and attack them at night. The GEE navigation aid and other equipment, such as bombsights, developed for Bomber Command, were also introduced into Coastal Command aircraft. Armour-piercing bombs, torpedoes and depth charges were developed to destroy enemy surface vessels and submarines. By 1943, with this improved equipment, Coastal Command began to have some real success in searching out and destroying submarines (U-boats), mine-sweepers (R-boats) and high-speed torpedo boats (E-boats). The Command also conducted successful air attacks against enemy convoys, ports and airfields.

However, the enemy had made huge gains on mainland Europe. April, May and June 1940 was a disastrous period during which time the Germans invaded and captured Norway, Holland, Belgium and northern France. Despite its equipment shortfalls, Coastal Command was heavily involved, flying a huge number of reconnaissance sorties and bombing raids along the whole theatre of war. The Command was also heavily involved in the evacuation of the British Army from Dunkirk, which began at the end of May. Nevertheless, by the end of June, the Germans had the whole coastline of north-west Europe under their control. The German Navy occupied the captured ports, which began to provide a safe haven for their ships and submarines, and the German Air Force occupied all the aerodromes along the occupied coastline whence they could mount offensive operations. Moreover, U-boats were decimating merchant ships that were bringing in essential supplies to the UK. The German war economy relied heavily on vital resources, such as iron-ore from Scandinavia, being shipped along the coast of north-west Europe in merchant vessels; the huge German merchant fleet was being used successfully to bring high-grade iron ore from Sweden via the Norwegian port of Narvik and into Rotterdam; from there it was transported by barge to the Ruhr to feed the German war industry.

After the fall of France, and the evacuation at Dunkirk, Coastal Command began an intensive campaign to bomb the enemy-occupied ports and airfields all along the occupied coastline. The bulk of the attacks concentrated on oil terminals, docks and harbours and the shipping in them. The ports that an invasion fleet might be expected to sail from were closely monitored by recon-naissance aircraft. The Command also continued its relentless 'search and destroy' missions against enemy shipping and submarines. It also attacked surface vessels that might carry cargoes used to feed the enemy war machine. This campaign was initially very costly in human life and aircraft, but became more successful from 1943 onwards when the command was equipped with more modern aircraft. Three main weapons were used in the attacks on enemy shipping: mines, bombs and torpedoes. Much of the action took place over the North Sea, particularly along the coastline of occupied Europe.

Docking was strategically well placed to contribute to these operations. The airfield hosted many squadrons that were dispersed from Bircham Newton to fly night operations over the North Sea and English Channel. Also, many visiting RAF and Fleet Air Arm squadrons were detached from other bases to use Docking as a forward base for offensive operations against enemy surface ships.

These squadrons also participated in the laying of mines and attacking ports, oil depots and airfields along the enemy-occupied coast, often at night. In addition, because of its location near the coast, Docking was often used as an emergency landing strip for aircraft returning flak-damaged, lost or short of fuel from operational sorties over the North Sea or from enemy-occupied Europe.

Docking was involved in far more operational activities than can be included in this short chapter. Nevertheless, some of the squadrons that flew from Docking and their operational activities are highlighted below.

No. 235 Squadron RAF

Bristol Blenheim aircraft of the type flown by No 235 Squadron

Number 235 Squadron, flying Blenheim IV aircraft and dispersed from Bircham Newton, was possibly the first operational squadron to use Docking airfield in the early summer of 1940. In early May 1940, 235 Squadron flew Coastal Command's first strikes against enemy shipping off the Dutch coast. This was quickly followed up with other shipping raids, reconnaissance and escort missions. Many aircraft had lucky escapes during these initial sorties, since Bf 109s often attacked them. Others were not so lucky and did not return. Some of the aircraft were detached to Detling in Kent and Thorney Island in Hampshire during May and June 1940 to cover the BEF retreat from Dunkirk. Later in the year, the squadron's twenty Blenheims took up full residence at Docking, and were employed in anti-shipping strikes, reconnaissance, anti-invasion patrols and convoy escort duties in the North Sea. The squadron departed in June 1941 to begin operations from Dyce in Scotland. Like most other Blenheim and Beaufort squadrons, they were eventually upgraded with the more powerful Beaufighter aircraft.

During 1940, several 235 Squadron Blenheims crashed at Bircham and in the surrounding countryside, including one at Docking, on 26 May 1940, when the aircraft spun into the ground out of cloud.

No 235 Squadron returned and was based at Docking from the end of May until the middle of July 1942, when it used its twenty Beaufighter Ic aircraft for anti-shipping operations off the Dutch coast.

Bristol Beaufighter similar to those flown by No. 235 Squadron

No. 22 Squadron RAF

Another squadron that used Docking in 1940 was 22 Squadron, flying Bristol Beaufort aircraft. In the early part of the war, this squadron was employed in mine-laying and anti-shipping torpedo operations. In order to cover as wide an area of the sea as possible, 22 Squadron aircraft were detached from their home base to many Coastal Command stations, including Bircham Newton (from May 1940 until March 1942) from where they were dispersed to Docking. When they were not mine-laying, codenamed 'Gardening' and mostly performed at night, the squadron flew 'Rover' patrols along the enemy-occupied coast seeking targets of opportunity, such as enemy shipping convoys.

In September 1940, two Beauforts crashed while landing at Docking. One was damaged beyond repair on 23rd September after stalling during a night landing and the other flew into the ground on 27 September on a night approach after being damaged by flak.

No. 206 Squadron RAF

Another squadron based at Bircham Newton, but also dispersed and flying operations out of Docking in 1940, was 206 Squadron, flying Anson and Hudson aircraft. Several operations in 1940 by 206 Squadron are described in *Norfolk Military Airfields* by Peter Walker, including attacks on motor torpedo boats in Boulogne harbour, attacks on a German destroyer and attacks on an enemy-occupied aerodrome.

The squadron was involved in flying patrols over the ships engaged in the evacuation of the British Expeditionary Force in May 1940, as is clear from the following extract from a citation to one of Bircham Newton's airmen, Flight Lieutenant Biddle, who was awarded the Distinguished Flying Cross.

37

'On 31 May 1940, whilst leading a flight of three Hudson aircraft on a patrol over the ships engaged in evacuating the British Expeditionary Force, this officer sighted a squadron of Skuas being attacked be eleven Messerschmitt 109s. The Skuas were hard pressed and two were shot down. Without hesitation and despite the fact that the Hudson is not a fighter aircraft, Flight Lieutenant Biddle led his flight against the enemy, damaging one Messerschmitt and causing the remainder to break off the engagement'

On 19 June 1940, Flt Lt Biddle piloted the Hudson that evacuated General Sikorski and his staff from Bordeaux to form the Polish army in England.

Rescue from the Skies, by Stephen Brewster Daniels, lists fifteen 206 Squadron Hudson crashes around the Bircham area in 1940, including three at Docking: in August an aircraft crashed near the airfield when it lost control in the circuit after take-off; in September another hit trees on take-off and belly-landed; and in October a third aircraft hit a hedge while landing and was damaged beyond repair.

The squadron moved from Bircham Newton to St Eval in Cornwall at the end of May 1941.

No. 500 (County of Kent) Squadron RAF

This squadron arrived at Bircham Newton with Anson and Blenheim IV aircraft in May 1941 to undertake reconnaissance and offensive operations over the North Sea. Many operations were flown from Docking. On 7 July, enemy aircraft shot one of the squadron aircraft down as it was landing at Docking at 0200 hours. The aircraft burnt out and the entire crew was killed.

While the squadron was at Bircham it flew a variety of missions, including anti-convoy sorties, dinghy searches and the more mundane inspection of floats and buoys. It also flew intruder missions into enemy-held territory. Aircraft M/500 conducted one such intruder sortie on 12 September, when the target was Schipol. The pilot crossed the Dutch coast at Noordwyk at 2152 hours. He then set course for Schipol, flying above the cloud at 13000 feet. When he arrived over the target, the cloud base was low and his starboard engine started to cut out. This added to an overheating port engine that had been occurring since he crossed the Dutch coast. To increase his misery, he was experiencing flak over the target area. Consequently, unable to sight his target, he set course for home, jettisoning his bombs over the sea. He landed back at base at 2340 hours. At the end of September the squadron had much greater success, when it bombed docks and shipyards at St Nazaire.

In mid-October, six Blenheims from 500 Squadron joined Hudsons from 407 and 59 squadrons in a combined anti-shipping patrol. They attacked an enemy convoy with some success, although they received flak from escort vessels.

No. 500 Squadron was subsequently upgraded with Hudson III and Hudson IV aircraft in November 1941. One of the Hudsons crashed on 1 December 1941, when it spun into the ground near the Docking to Choseley road after a night take-off from Docking. The crew of six all died. Several 500 Squadron Hudsons crashed in Norfolk in 1942, including two that were lost on the same day at Docking on 8 February. One aircraft crash-landed and the other stalled during an overshoot, killing the crew of four. The squadron left Bircham Newton for Stornoway in March 1942.

No. 225 Squadron

From July 1941 until August 1942, a detachment of 225 Squadron aircraft was based at Docking. This was an Army Cooperation Unit supporting or cooperating with the British Army. The pilots of army cooperation units traditionally flew a variety of missions including reconnaissance, artillery spotting, communication and tactical liaison between RAF ground attack aircraft and army troops. However, at Docking, the detachment flew armed recon-naissance patrols over the North Sea. Initially 225 Squadron was equipped with Westland Lysander Mk III aircraft, but it was augmented by Hawker Hurricane Mk I and North American Mustang Mk I aircraft during 1942. The Lysanders, affectionately known as 'tin Lizzies', were used mainly for target towing and air-sea rescue duties, dropping rubber dinghies and supplies to 'ditched' aircrew.

The Westland Lysander aircraft of the type flown by No. 225 Squadron

No. 241 and No. 268 Squadrons

Detachments from these two Army Cooperation squadrons flew from Docking in 1941 and 1942 using Curtiss Tomahawk Mk. II A aircraft. 241 Squadron arrived in August 1941 and 268 Squadron arrived in December 1941. Following a period flying armed reconnaissance patrols off the Dutch coast, both detachments departed in May 1942.

No. 320 (Dutch) Squadron RAF

Following the invasion of the Netherlands in May 1940, many airmen from the Royal Dutch Naval Air Service (DNAS) escaped to Britain, forming the nucleus of 320 (Dutch) Squadron, which was formed at Pembroke Dock in June 1940 and placed within Coastal Command. They were deployed to Bircham Newton with their Hudson aircraft from April 1942 until March 1943. The squadron often undertook 'Rover' patrols, which were low-level searches for suitable shipping targets conducted by two or three aircraft. They attacked enemy shipping

Hudson aircraft attacking shipping with its bomb doors open

with machine guns and with bombs. Many of their anti-shipping operations off the Netherlands coast were conducted with 407 (Demon) Squadron RCAF, which was also at Bircham Newton at this time. The two squadrons were on standby to take off once a reconnaissance aircraft had reported an enemy convoy. Both squadrons gained a fearful reputation for attacking enemy shipping at mast height or lower, in an attempt to avoid the enemy flak.

Towards the end of its tenure at Bircham Newton and Docking, 320 Squadron flew some combined operations with a second Canadian squadron, 415 (Swordfish) Squadron, which was using Docking as a forward base in early 1943.

This Hudson sortie, conducted by aircraft V-Victor on 30 May 1942, and recorded in the Operations Record Book, provides an insight into a typical night operation conducted by the squadron. The pilot took off at 23:00 hrs and formed up with the other squadron aircraft to fly across the North Sea. They subsequently sighted an enemy convoy north of the Frisian Islands. The convoy of about seven ships had at least eight escort vessels and consequently the aircraft encountered heavy flak from all sides. The pilot of Hudson V-Victor selected a target, which he described as a tug-type with a tall mast and high bridge, forward of the funnel. He attacked the vessel at mast height, dropping ten bombs. The rear gunner observed an explosion on the deck amidships, and the vessel was seen to burst into flames. V-Victor experienced heavy flak from a shore battery and from the convoy at the time of the attack. Also the aircrew spotted enemy aircraft, possibly a Ju 88, and took evasive action. As soon as possible, the pilot set course for Cromer and dashed back across the North Sea, landing at Docking at 02:45 hrs. There were similar reports from other squadron pilots who participated in this attack. Of the six aircraft that participated in this operation, two failed to return, including the one piloted by the squadron leader.

Despite the danger, aircraft from the 320 Squadron and other squadrons often landed with their flares and bombs on board if they didn't sight their targets. For example, a Hudson of 320 Squadron took off for an anti-shipping (NOMAD) patrol on the evening of 13 February. A full patrol was carried out, but no enemy shipping was sighted. Consequently, the aircraft returned to Docking, landing after midnight with its bombs on board.

Daring anti-shipping operations conducted by 320 Squadron off the Dutch coast from Docking in May 1942 are well documented in Andrew Hendrie's *Lockheed Hudson in World War II* and other sources. The squadron also participated in the '1000 Bomber' raid on Bremen in June 1942. In March 1943, the squadron was transferred to Bomber Command and started to re-equip with Mitchell aircraft.

Bombing up a Hudson prior to an operational mission

During its period with Coastal Command, 320 Squadron had carried out over 1200 operational flights and had damaged or destroyed thirty-seven enemy ships. However, the squadron lost over one third of their Hudson aircraft. Losses of crews were very high during 320 Squadron's stay at Bircham Newton and Docking, particularly in the period April to July 1942.

41

No. 407 (Demon) Squadron RCAF

No. 407 Squadron was the first of two Canadian squadrons to fly from Docking. Equipped with Hudson aircraft, the squadron was based at Bircham Newton from March until September 1942, replacing No. 500 Squadron, and flew night operations from Docking. The squadron's main task was to seek out and destroy enemy shipping. It earned its 'Demon' nickname because of its tenacity at carrying out these mast-height attacks on enemy convoys off the Frisian Islands and Dutch coast. It was acclaimed as one of the most successful strike squadrons in Coastal Command, with a record of 83,000 tons of shipping sunk or damaged in a single month. As if to demonstrate the squadron's prowess at low flying, one pilot, Pilot Officer Larry O'Connell, left one of his bomb doors hanging on the mast of a ship he attacked.

These words, taken from a poem written by a 407 Squadron wireless operator/air gunner in 1942, gives an impression of low-level attacks against enemy convoys:

'Bomb doors open, throttle wide,
Approaching from the starboard side.
Below their mast-height on we sped,
The flak was flashing o'er our head.

Upward we flew into the night,
'Bombs gone!' the call came with delight,
Downward we flew when we were past,
The danger from the rising mast.'

With mast-height bombing, the bombs did not explode on contact. Instead, there was a ten-second delay to allow the aircraft to get clear of the scene.

Anti-shipping strikes conducted by 407 Squadron are documented in many of the books listed at the end of this book. Twelve aircraft conducted a very successful attack on an enemy convoy off the Dutch coast on 7 May 1942. This attack was conducted against heavily-defended surface vessels in semi-darkness at heights below mast level. Seven ships were hit and damaged by bombs and all of the aircraft returned to base, although some were heavily damaged. Fortunately, none of the aircrew was wounded.

The squadron flew combined operations with 320 (Dutch) Squadron, which was also using Docking for night operations at this time. Crews from the two squadrons, usually six from each, were placed on standby at Docking awaiting reports of enemy convoys. Once a reconnaissance aircraft reported a suitable convoy, the aircraft would take off to attack it. One or more aircraft would fly ahead to drop flares to illuminate the target, which the others would attack at mast height, flying over the convoy and releasing their bombs. The two squadrons flew on these dangerous missions on a daily basis, sustaining huge losses, which peaked in the period from April to July 1942.

407 Squadron airmen near their Hudson

A particularly costly joint mission against a German convoy off the Dutch coast on 15 May 1942 is well documented in several references. From a total of 11 aircraft participating in the mission, only 4 returned safely. 407 Squadron bore the brunt of the casualties. One aircraft, V-Victor, that had been badly damaged by enemy gunfire crashed near RAF Coningsby, killing all of the crew. Another aircraft, O-Orange, whose pilot was wounded in his hands, arms and leg, arrived back at Docking with severe damage. As the wounded pilot was making his approach, both engines failed and the aircraft crashed onto a gun pit at the edge of the airfield, killing an army AA gunner. One of the crew was killed and the other two were seriously wounded with a broken collarbone and fractured spine, respectively. Another aircraft, K-King, whose instruments and hydraulics had been rendered useless by enemy gunfire, made a successful belly landing at Docking. Similarly, aircraft W-William was brought safely back to Docking despite heavy damage. In the pursuit of this particular mission, twenty-two 407 Squadron aircrew were killed and four were seriously injured. In addition to these huge losses, many of the returning aircraft were so seriously damaged that they were of no further use to the squadron.

Faced with these huge losses, which rose to at least three aircraft lost for every ship that was sunk, Coastal Command was forced to abandon low-level attacks, and begin bombing at a higher level. In his book, *Canadian Squadrons in Coastal Command,* Andrew Hendrie describes several 407 Squadron operations flown from Docking during the period May through September 1942, including some flown at high level in conjunction with Nos. 59 Squadron RAF, 320 Dutch Squadron, 415 Squadron RCAF and FAA Swordfish squadrons. In one of these operations, conducted on 25 August and led by the squadron CO, Wing Commander Brown, a high-level attack was made against a convoy sighted off the Frisian Islands. The aircraft released flares to illuminate their targets, which were then attacked with 1000 pound bombs. One pilot described how he scored a direct hit on one of the ships, causing a large column of black smoke. He was, however, picked up and chased by enemy aircraft on his way back to base. Flying into low cloud and heavy rainfall, he made contact with the English coastline near North Coates in Lincolnshire. He flew south at very low altitude following the coastline, eventually landing at Docking in a blinding rainstorm at 01:10 hrs. Andrew Hendrie also describes a daring raid made by a 407 Squadron pilot on the heavily defended Den Helder harbour. Apparently the pilot had been searching for a convoy off the Dutch coast. Unable to locate any enemy shipping, he decided to bomb the docks at Den Helder, where it was thought that he demolished a large factory, a torpedo dump, and a ship in the harbour before he returned to Docking, landing in a heavy rainstorm just before midnight. It was reported that RAF bomber crews could see the Den Helder fires from fifty miles away.

From November 1942 Coastal Command adopted Strike Wing tactics for anti-shipping operations, using mixed variants of the Beaufighter aircraft, including fighters and bombers to neutralize the deadly flak ships and torpedo-carrying Torbeaus. Combined anti-shipping strikes by a sizeable mixed force of aircraft became the norm from 1943 onwards.

407 Squadron left Bircham Newton for St Eval in Cornwall in late September 1942.

However, in November 1942, it was re-assembled at Docking for conversion training on Wellington aircraft, which were to replace the squadron's Hudsons. The Hudsons were by then considered seriously under-armed for attacks against enemy convoys and submarines. Nevertheless, while at Docking in January 1943, 407 Squadron was still operating Hudsons on strikes off the Dutch coast in combination with 320 Squadron. The two squadrons were credited with the sinking of a merchant vessel *Algeria* of 1619 tons following a successful raid on 18 January. Two days later, one of 407 Squadron's aircraft was lost on a reconnaissance sortie near the Dutch coast.

However, by late January 1943, the squadron was equipped with Wellington XI aircraft and began its conversion training. The Wellingtons were equipped with nose and tail gun turrets. To locate surface vessels and submarines, many Coastal Command aircraft, including the Wellingtons, were equipped with Air to Surface Vessel (ASV) radar and anti-submarine bombs or depth charges. Early versions of the Wellington carried ASV radar masts on top of the fuselage and were nicknamed 'Stickleback' Wellingtons. However, later marks of the aircraft housed the ASV radar in a chin radome beneath its nose. Initially they dropped flares to illuminate any detected surface vessel or submarine, but these were unreliable. Consequently, an airborne searchlight, the Leigh Light, was developed for the Wellington. A Wellington crew consisted of the pilot, co-pilot, navigator, and up to three wireless operator/air gunners. The Wellington would fly on its anti-shipping operations at night at low level (approximately 1000 feet). The wireless operators would use the ASV radar to scan the surface of the sea for surface vessels or U-boats that would have surfaced to charge their batteries.

In the following month 407 Squadron moved on to Skitten, near Wick in Scotland, to continue Wellington conversion training and anti-submarine patrols, before returning to its home base at Chivenor in Devon.

No 811, 812 and 819 Squadrons of the Fleet Air Arm

Naval aircraft also flew from Docking. Several Fleet Air Arm (FAA) squadrons were loaned to RAF Coastal Command during WW2. During the period August to December 1942, Nos 811, 812 and 819 FAA squadrons flew from Docking on night operations over the North Sea using Fairey Swordfish aircraft, which they called 'Stringbags'. The Swordfish squadrons carried out many successful operations with No. 320 (Dutch) Squadron and 407 (Demon) Squadron, who also flew night operations from Docking using Hudson aircraft. The Hudsons would be armed with 250-pounder bombs and the Swordfish with torpedoes. Sometimes one or more of the Swordfish aircraft would drop flares to illuminate the targets for the other attacking aircraft. The Swordfish often carried out the entire missions at very low altitudes to avoid detection. Torpedo attacks would be made at wave-top levels of under 100 feet.

To attack targets that were outside their range from Docking, the Swordfish aircraft would be flown at dusk down to a base in southern England, such as Manston, returning to Norfolk on the following morning. In an attempt to increase their range, long-range tanks were fitted to 811 Squadron's Swordfish aircraft at Docking, but they were removed a few weeks later when it was agreed that they made the aircraft unstable and unsafe. Controversially, the long-range tanks had also displaced the telegraphist air-gunner (TAG), who normally flew as part of the crew.

Fairey Swordfish of the type flown by FAA Squadrons from Docking

45

A typical combined operation was conducted on the night of 4 September 1942, when five Hudsons of 320 Squadron and eight Hudsons of 407 Squadron took off from Docking with four Swordfish of 819 Squadron to attack the Italian ore ship *Africana* and her escorts off the coast of northern France. One of the Swordfish aircraft located the enemy convoy and dropped flares to illuminate the target, which was then attacked with torpedoes by two other Swordfish aircraft. However, no results were confirmed, except for large spouts of water seen erupting amongst the ships. Some of the Hudson aircraft also attempted to attack the convoy with bombs, but were driven off by enemy aircraft and heavy flak, some of which came from Dunkerque. One Hudson managed to release its bombs, which were seen to fall some distance from an escort vessel. Two days later 320, 407 and 819 Squadrons carried out another operation against targets off Dunkerque and the Frisian Islands, flying from Docking and Manston.

The CO of 811 Squadron, Lt Cdr H.S. Hayes RN, had been a prisoner of war in Sweden after ditching in a lake following attacks on enemy shipping at Tromso in 1940 as a member of 801 Squadron. Apparently his aircraft was hit by anti-aircraft fire, and since he was unable to find his aircraft carrier, he ditched in Lake Vassara, near Gallivare in Sweden. He was subsequently captured and interned in Sweden. It is not known how he gained his freedom prior to bringing 811 Squadron to Docking. Some of the operations flown from Docking by No. 811 Squadron are well documented by one of their ex-pilots, John Godley (later to become Lord Kilbracken), in *Bring Back my Stringbag*.

These operations included laying mines off the Dutch coast. These were set to explode when the magnetic fields of enemy shipping passed within their range. They also laid mines at the approaches to enemy-occupied harbours such as Le Havre. For anti-shipping operations with torpedoes, when each aircraft was given a search zone, the slow speed and relative short range of the Swordfish was a great disadvantage. Sometimes the aircraft flew to a forward base at Ludham, north-east of Norwich, to get fifty miles closer to their targets off the Frisian Islands. For example, on 26 September, Hudsons of 320 Squadron took off from Docking and Swordfish aircraft from 811 and 812 squadrons took off from Ludham to attack enemy shipping off the Frisian Islands.

The slow speed of the Swordfish made them very vulnerable to enemy fighter aircraft, such as the ME-109. However, despite these disadvantages, the 'stringbags' were successful in several attacks against enemy convoys, often encountered on the limits of their range.

No. 304 (Polish) Squadron RAF

This Polish Squadron had its first encounter with Docking in June 1942 when selected crews flew their Wellington Ic bombers to Docking from their base at Dale in South Wales to be refuelled and bombed up in preparation for the '1000 Bomber' raid on Bremen, which will be described later. One of the squadron's aircraft did not return from the raid.

During 1942 and early 1943 No. 304 (Polish) Squadron had built up a good reputation for its anti-submarine operations in the Bay of Biscay. However, at the end of March 1943, No. 304 Squadron was transferred to 18 Group of Coastal Command and relocated to Docking to be re-equipped with Wellington Mk X aircraft. They were to become a torpedo-carrying squadron with a new anti-shipping role. Fortunately, after two months of extensive training at Docking and elsewhere, it was realized that the Wellington aircraft was not suited to this role. Consequently, No. 304 Squadron was transferred back to 19 Group to continue their anti-submarine patrols in the Bay of Biscay.

Two of No. 304 Squadron's Wellingtons crashed on landing at Docking in April 1943 and May 1943 respectively.

During their stay at Docking, 304 Squadron personnel of all ranks, both aircrew and ground, took part in a defence exercise at the airfield, in which members of the Scots Guards were employed as an attacking force.

**Wellington GR Mk XIV in service with 304 (Polish) Squadron
at Docking, 1943**

The '1000 Bomber' Raid on Bremen

A '1000 Bomber' raid on Bremen on the night of 25/26 June 1942 was laid on by Bomber Command but included 20 Wellington and 82 Hudson aircraft from Coastal Command, some of which flew from Docking. These were 11 Hudson aircraft from No. 407 (Demon) Squadron and 6 Hudsons from No. 320 (Dutch) Squadron. Also, 7 Wellington aircraft from No. 304 (Polish) Squadron and 13 Wellington aircraft from No. 311 (Czecho-Slovak) Squadron participated. As previously mentioned, No. 304 (Polish) Squadron had flown into Docking in preparation for the raid from its home base at Dale in South Wales. Similarly, No. 311 Squadron was a temporary visitor from Aldergrove in Northern Ireland. No. 311 Squadron had been formed from Czech Air Force personnel who had

47

previously met in France but had escaped to this country at the time of the French collapse in 1940. It began life as part of Bomber Command, but was transferred to Coastal Command in April 1942.

The targets in this 1000 Bomber raid were the docks and submarine base at Bremen plus a Focke-Wulf factory with its airfield and nearby oil refineries. Although the raid was deemed successful, 49 RAF aircraft were destroyed and 64 were damaged with a considerable loss of life. All of the No. 407 Squadron Hudsons returned from the raid, although six of them didn't reach the target because of fuel shortages and most of the aircraft sustained flak damage. One Hudson from No. 320 Squadron did not return from the raid. Also, one of the No. 304 Squadron Wellingtons was shot down in the raid, killing all the crew. One of the Wellingtons from No. 311 Squadron crashed on Brancaster beach, but fortunately the crew survived.

No. 143 Squadron RAF

No. 143 Squadron came to Docking for one month in July 1942 to change its Blenheims for Beaufighters. The squadron flew a few anti-shipping patrols over the North Sea before departing to RAF North Coates in late August. The Beaufighter became a remarkably successful and powerful long-range fighter and torpedo bomber for Coastal Command. North Coates, in Lincolnshire, subsequently became the home of the 'North Coates Strike Wing' consisting of two squadrons of Beaufighter torpedo bombers, which had great success in attacking enemy shipping.

No. 53 Squadron RAF

No. 53 Squadron first flew from Docking in the period July to October 1941 using Hudson aircraft to patrol the Dutch coast and protect coastal convoys. The squadron returned again in January 1943 to exchange its Hudson aircraft for twenty Armstrong Whitworth Whitley GR VII aircraft, which had longer range and were equipped with ASV radar. After a period training on the new aircraft, 53 Squadron departed for Thorney Island at the end of April.

No. 415 (Swordfish) Squadron RCAF

During the period from 1941 to 1943 this Canadian squadron had flown Handley-Page Hampden aircraft in a torpedo bomber role at various Coastal Command stations, including Thorney Island, St Eval, North Coates, Wick and Leuchars. The squadron first used Docking as an advanced base for anti-shipping operations using Hampden I torpedo bombers in early 1943. The Coastal Command Order of Battle (ORBAT) for 10 May 1943 indicates that 15 Hampdens were available at Docking, on detachment from Thorney Island.

The Hampden was of all-metal construction. Its fuselage had a deep forward body, housing the crew, and a slender tail boom carrying the tail-plane and twin fins and rudders. It was nicknamed 'the flying suitcase' because of its cramped crew positions, and it suffered heavy losses from enemy fighters when it was first used in daylight raids against Germany. Consequently, it was withdrawn from Bomber Command operations and refitted with heavier armament and armour. It was later used in night bombing missions and some were transferred to Coastal Command, where it was converted for use as a torpedo bomber and as meteorological reconnaissance aircraft. 521 Squadron used the Hampden at Docking in this latter role. The cramped crew positions led to fatigue on long flights and made it almost impossible for the crew to gain access to each other or to escape from the aircraft in an emergency. Consequently, many airmen lost their lives in Hampdens during take-offs and crash landings at Docking.

415 (Swordfish) Squadron conducted some combined operations with No. 320 (Dutch) Squadron, which was still flying night operations from Docking in early 1943. One such combined operation was conducted on 18 February 1943 with disastrous consequences. Six Hampdens from the Canadian squadron and nine Hudsons from the Dutch squadron were to attack an enemy convoy that had been sighted off Ijmuiden. The aircraft were to take off from Docking, beginning at 2020 hrs. The aircraft of No. 320 Squadron had mixed success at attacking the convoy, but all returned safely. One Hudson, which was airborne at 2030 hrs, quickly developed large flames from its starboard engine and had to return, after jettisoning its bombs in the sea. Five of the Hudsons located the convoy and attacked with their bombs. Two aircraft scored direct hits, and two missed their target. The aircrew of one returning aircraft reported that their bombs had 'hung up'. Since they were unsuccessful at jettisoning the bombs, they landed back at Docking with all weapons on board.

The Hampdens of 415 Squadron did not fare as well. Three aircraft failed to get airborne for unspecified reasons, and one crashed on take off near Docking station, bursting into flames with no survivors. The police had to evacuate nearby houses because of an unexploded torpedo on board this ill-fated aircraft. One successful Hampden sortie sighted enemy ships and released a torpedo, but the results were not observed. Three other aircraft returned without sighting the convoy, and one failed to return. The latter was believed to have ditched in the sea.

Another Hampden loss was experienced a few days later, on 21 February 1943. Hampden O/415 was airborne at Docking at 2039 hrs on an offensive search and destroy mission. At 2200 hrs the pilot sighted flares and flak. Shortly afterwards, through the haze, he spotted several enemy surface vessels, which he attacked, scoring a hit on the bow of one vessel. He then had to take evasive action as he was targeted by violent flak. The Hampden was hit and badly damaged and was ditched in the sea at 2257 hrs. However, all of the crew were successfully rescued by a Walrus aircraft and landed safely at Martlesham Heath.

Fairey Albacore as used by No. 415 Squadron

In November 1943 the squadron was sent back to Bircham Newton partially re-equipped with Wellington VIII (fitted with Leigh Light). The squadron also flew Albacore biplanes, mainly from Manston and Thorney Island. The Albacore, designed as a replacement for the Fairey Swordfish 'Stringbag', was the last operational biplane to be used by the RCAF and the only one to be used in action. It carried a crew of two and could carry 350 lb bombs or a torpedo. Although the Albacore aircraft were usually detached to Manston, they sometimes operated from Docking. In his book *Canadian Strike Squadrons in Coastal Command,* Andrew Hendrie describes an Albacore sortie flown from Docking in February 1944. The aircraft, piloted by F/O Chadwick, was airborne from Docking at 0100 hrs and an hour later was attacking enemy vessels off Boulogne. Although he was initially unable to see any targets, Chadwick was homed to the enemy ships by his navigator using ASV radar. He released six bombs from an altitude of 800 feet, which resulted in a direct hit on one vessel, which was claimed as destroyed.

The squadron, divided into two Flights, now had an established strength of 10 Wellingtons and 20 Albacores. The role of the Wellington Flight was to seek out enemy shipping at night, report their sightings to headquarters, to home any strike forces sent out onto the targets, and to illuminate the targets for attack by the strike forces. The Wellingtons would normally attack targets only when operating independently.

ASV radar and the GEE navigation equipment were used to find and plot the position of enemy craft. The GEE equipment fixed the aircraft's position from radio emissions from three ground stations. These were displayed as blips on grid lines across a radar screen. GEE coordinates could then be transferred to charts to establish the ground position, which, relayed to headquarters staff, enabled them to dispatch surface forces and strike aircraft to attack the enemy craft. The Wellingtons would continue to shadow the target, and whenever possible guide the strike forces towards the target using radio transmission R/T. They would also illuminate the targets, where appropriate, using their Leigh Light or flares. The Albacores, operating under the control of 11 Group would normally operate on dark nights only, being vectored to their targets to make dive attacks with 250 lb bombs.

Like many other Bircham squadrons, 415 Squadron (Wellington Flight) was dispersed and flew its night operations from Docking. It was decided in this case that the servicing personnel (fitters, riggers and others) would work and be quartered at Docking. They often complained because they worked in the remote dispersal areas and had long distances to walk or cycle between their work, their billets and the mess. The officers had accommodation at Bircham Newton and were ferried to and from Docking.

The squadron soon became expert in tracking down and destroying German E-boats in cooperation with the navy. E-boats were a menace to allied shipping. They were powered by diesel engines, had a low profile and were extremely fast. Under the cover of darkness, they would leave the sanctuary of their continental ports and attack enemy shipping off the east coast. No. 415 Squadron flew numerous anti-shipping patrols at night across the North Sea in what was known as 'Operation Deadly', trying to locate surface craft, such as E-boats, using ASV radar. This seems to have been a frustrating task. Frequently radar 'blips' would be picked up but quickly lost again before the target could be illuminated by flares or flame floats. Many sorties had to be aborted because of equipment failure. The Wellington aircraft would attempt to find and illuminate targets for its Albacore aircraft or naval vessels to attack and destroy. However, there are numerous entries in the Operations Record Book for late 1943 and the first half of 1944 of the form 'Airborne Docking on anti E-boat patrol in cooperation with navy', with no mention of any contacts. On occasions when the squadron was successful, it would illuminate the target and send a message back to base requesting naval forces to attack it.

Wellington aircraft of No. 415 Squadron employing ASV radar

The following example (with times omitted) illustrates a successful operation.

14/2/44 Wellington D: 'Airborne Docking on anti E-boat patrol with navy. 'E' boats located and messages sent to base. Engagement between surface forces followed. 1 'E' boat sunk, 3 or 4 'E' boats damaged. Our casualties were light. Landed Docking'

The squadron also flew long-range patrols carrying bombs to locate and attack enemy convoys and was successful in sinking several ships. Often, after long searches, no convoys would be detected, and some bombs would have to be jettisoned prior to landing back at Docking. The following example illustrates such a sortie (with times omitted).

25/3/44 Wellington H: 'Airborne Docking loaded with 5 X 500 lb bombs to patrol convoy route off Dutch coast for any enemy convoys. Patrol completed 5 times, but no convoy sighted. Jettisoned three bombs as ordered before landing at Docking'

No. 415 Squadron Wellington crew in 1944

In 'Operation Gilbey', which began in January 1944, the squadron also dropped flares to illuminate targets for Torbeau aircraft from the North Coates Wing. The Torbeau was a version of the Beaufighter that was modified to drop torpedoes. On receipt of a reconnaissance report of an enemy convoy, a flare-carrying Wellington was used to relocate the target and drop flame floats and also marine markers parallel to the convoy's course. The marine markers indicated to the strike force the track it had to follow to find the target. The Wellington would also drop sufficient flares over the target to give the Torbeaus enough illumination to make their attack. The first big success using this technique occurred on the night of 5/6 March 1944, when a Wellington from 415 Squadron found a small convoy off the Dutch coast. Four Beaufighters were sent to the last reported position of the convoy and launched an attack with torpedoes assisted by the flare illumination laid down by the Wellington. The Wellington also dropped its 500-lb bombs on the convoy. Torpedoes and bombs found their targets and the main vessel, *Diana*, of almost 2000 tons, was sunk. 415 Squadron further developed the Gilbey tactics using their Wellingtons in combination with their torpedo-carrying Albacore aircraft and was successful in seriously damaging an Italian vessel of more than 4,000 tons on the night of 23/24 March. One of the squadron's most successful operations occurred on 24 May 1944, when its Albacore aircraft successfully sank the infamous German torpedo boat *Grief*.

The squadron later flew night patrols in connection with the preparations for the invasion of Normandy. In the actual D-Day operations, the squadron assisted in the laying of smoke screens for the allied naval forces.

Four 415 Squadron Hampden aircraft crashed at Docking in 1943 during take-offs and landings. The squadron flew its final night searches from Docking on 20 July 1944, when No. 524 Squadron began to take over its aircraft and anti-shipping tasks. The Canadian 415 Squadron was then transferred from Coastal to Bomber Command, although its Albacore aircraft and many of the aircrew were transferred to No. 119 (RAF) Squadron at Bircham Newton.

No. 524 Squadron RAF

In July 1944, No 524 Squadron replaced 415 (Swordfish) Squadron, flying Wellington GR XIII aircraft. The squadron undertook patrols to locate and illuminate enemy shipping off the Dutch coast. They also bombed E-boats and other targets using flare lights. The squadron flew from Docking until October 1944, when it moved to Langham because Docking became waterlogged. It was disbanded at Langham in June 1945.

No. 854 and 854 Squadron FAA

During 1944, No 157 General Reconnaissance Wing was formed within Coastal Command from 854 and 855 squadrons of the Fleet Air Arm. Avenger aircraft from 855 Squadron flew from Docking in the period May to September 1944, carrying out patrols looking for enemy shipping in the North Sea. In September 1944, the squadron moved to Bircham Newton.

Emergency Landings and Crashes

Many aircraft from other RAF stations used Docking as an emergency landing strip when they were returning, damaged or low on fuel, from operations over occupied Europe. In the early morning of 9 October 1940, an Armstrong

Whitworth Whitley bomber, which had flown from Linton-on-Ouse on a bombing raid on Germany, crashed and burnt out about ½ mile east of Docking church whilst attempting an emergency landing. All 5 crew members were killed. On 18 August 1942, a Stirling bomber returning from operations over mainland Europe and seriously damaged by flak crash landed on the airfield. Another such crash landing was attempted on 1 May 1943 by the pilot of a Handley Page Halifax, which had taken off from Linton-on-Ouse late in the previous evening for an attack on Essen. Damaged by flak, it crashed early in the morning while attempting an emergency landing at Docking. The Australian sergeant pilot and five of his crew were killed and two were injured in this incident. The pilot had been awarded the DFM less than one month earlier for successfully flying his damaged aircraft back from a previous raid over Germany.

Many more forced landings occurred at Docking as the war progressed, including Lancaster aircraft returning from bombing operations, either damaged, lost or short of fuel. For example, on 17 January, five Lancasters from various bomber squadrons made emergency landings at Docking after a large raid on Berlin. On 18 March, a Halifax from 102 Squadron landed at Docking to get the rear gunner into hospital. The aircraft had been on a bombing mission to Essen, but was attacked by enemy aircraft on the run in to the target. The unfortunate rear gunner had been wounded in the face and leg. On 5 April, a Wellington belonging to 432 Squadron landed at Docking, short of fuel after visiting Kiel. On 5 May, yet another Lancaster landed after attacking the Rhine and experiencing serious problems with two of its engines. The dawn scene at Docking must often have been very surprising to its resident airmen, with strange aircraft scattered around the various dispersals.

Three Mosquito aircraft crashed at Docking during WW2: On 16 March 1943, the first one, belonging to No. 139 Squadron, crash landed on returning from operations over Europe; on 21 May 1945, a second aircraft, belonging to No. 1 Prep Pool, overshot the runway and dropped out of control; and on 8 July 1945, a third Mosquito, belonging to the Bomber Support Development Unit (BDSU) from Swanton Morley, broke up in mid air and crashed on the airfield.

5. Other Operations

Beam Approach Training

No 22 BAT Flight, which became No.1522 BAT Flight was formed at Docking in October 1941 and was based there until April 1942 flying Airspeed Oxford Mk I aircraft, which was a twin-engined training monoplane, nicknamed the 'Ox-Box'. On 16 July 1942 No. 1525 Beam Approach Training Flight moved to Docking from Brize Norton and stayed until it was disbanded at the end of June 1945. The Flight was equipped with eight Oxford Mk Is and was responsible for training Coastal Command pilots in the use of a WW2 navigation aid, called Standard Beam Approach (S.B.A), installed on most large RAF airfields. Using this system, in bad visibility when there was no diversion airfield available, pilots could make semi-blind landings using radio beams on the approach to the runway.

Airspeed Oxford of the type used by the BAT Flight at Docking

S.B.A was a radio transmitter sited in line with the runway to transmit a signal in a narrow beam along and beyond the runway. It was an audible system, with the pilot hearing the beam as a steady note in his earphones, called 'the beam'. On either side of the beam, the transmitter transmitted a different Morse code signal. For simplicity, we will assume that the pilot received an audible signal of Morse code 'dashes' if he was on one side of the beam and Morse code 'dots' if he was on the opposite side. In between these Morse signals and the beam, the pilot heard the codes superimposed over the steady note of the beam, telling him that he was in the 'twilight zone', and that he had almost reached the beam. This helped him to adjust his turn and avoid passing through 'the beam' into the opposite side. Two marker beacons helped the pilot to judge his distance from the runway. These were low-powered transmitters, which produced yet more audible signals in the pilot's earphones. The outer marker beacon was usually positioned about two miles from the airfield and the inner marker beacon near the end of the runway.

Landing using the beam was a very tricky and dangerous business. It required very accurate flying and timing, often entirely blind, and concentration on the instruments and signals being heard. It also involved following a number of standard procedures in close coordination with the control tower. Consequently, rigorous training was essential.

The following poem, which appeared in *TEE EMM*, the wartime Air Ministry monthly training magazine, sums up the difficulties of landing with S.B.A.

> Is it a dot? Or is it a dash? What does the 'kicker' say?
> Do we come? Or do we go? Are we so far away?
> Nothing ever seems to tell just what it ought to say,
> When first attempts are being made, to cope with S.B.A.!
> In and out the twilight, up and down the beam,
> Dashes, dots and beacons are never what they seem.
> Is the aerial up, or down? Inter-com or mix?
> Volume weak, or volume strong? What a box of tricks!
> First along the Q.D.M. Then the Q.D.R.
> Plus or minus, more or less, near and yet so far!
> Big corrections into wind, small the other way,
> Counting more or counting less, add or take away
> Sitting in a pool of sweat, trying might and main;
> Drift has changed with loss of height, round we go again.
> Gremlins rap the Perspex, thoughts flow thick and fast,
> Stick to the Sperry panel, or those thoughts may be your last!
> Subconsciously, yet so precise, how easy when you know,
> Reactions are so rapid now, where once they were so slow.
> So now you fly in Q.B.I. and, whereas, in the past,
> You scraped above the undergrowth, now through the overcast.

The records of No. 1525 BAT Flight show that it quickly became operational at Docking in July 1942, and began a very intensive S.B.A training programme that lasted for the remainder of the war. However, some early interruptions and mishaps are worth noting. On 27 July 1942, training was interrupted by the presence of hostile aircraft, which resulted in all aircraft being grounded. Bombs subsequently hit the airfield, but there were no casualties amongst the flight personnel or trainees. Training was interrupted for a second time by the presence of hostile aircraft on the 2 August, but again no casualties or damage was sustained.

In August 1942 two incidents resulted in serious aircraft damage. An aircraft on the ground was struck by a drogue released from a towing Lysander, holing the main plane. A few days later, a student retracted the undercarriage of one of the aircraft whilst on the ground with its engines running, resulting in serious (Cat 'A') damage to the aircraft. Another aircraft sustained serious damage in November 1942 when it attempted to land in very poor visibility. Luckily, no casualties resulted from these incidents.

The worst accident suffered by 1525 BAT Flight occurred on 16 January 1944, when one of the Oxfords crashed near Docking railway station. The aircraft struck trees when approaching the airfield on beam in very bad weather; the crew of three was killed in this accident. One of the crew, 2nd Lt J. M. Wright of the SAAF, was buried at Great Bircham. A second crew-member, F/O J.R. Galbraith of the RCAF, was buried nearby at Hunstanton.

One of the biggest hazards to the training programme appears to have been the weather. There was frequent loss of flying because of thick fog, perhaps because of Docking's position near the coast. Also, the airfield became waterlogged after heavy rain. The airfield seems to have become almost unusable in November and December 1944, when there was only one landing strip available for much of the time. Consequently, the pilots had to spend more time on the link trainer. Just to make matters worse, the airfield was covered in snow in January 1945. To make up for lost time, S.B.A training was conducted during daylight and at night in February 1945.

No. 2 Armament Practice Camp

Starting in August 1944, No. 2 Armament Practice Camp was based at Docking for a period, employing Westland Lysander and Miles Martinet aircraft in target towing tasks. Crews that were undergoing a gunnery course would attend lectures and fly live firing exercises. In the Hudson and Ventura, for example, the WOp/AGs would be expected to fire from the turret at a drogue being towed by the target-towing aircraft. The pilot, on the other hand, would be expected to engage a fixed target on a beach, or one being towed behind a launch at sea, using his fixed forward-facing guns in the nose of his aircraft. Some target-towing launches were moored at Wells-next-the-Sea for this purpose. Tracer shells would be inserted at intervals along the belts of ammunition, making the stream of shells visible, to assist in sighting the target. The Martinet would tow a target drogue at about 150 knots, usually much slower than the attacking aircraft. Consequently the attacking aircraft would follow the Martinet on a parallel track while the WOp/AG attempted to get the target drogue in his gunsight, while avoiding the towing aircraft. Target-towing was clearly not an occupation for the weak-hearted. Spare a thought for the target drogue operator who sat in the rear seat of some towing aircraft, closest to the drogue target. He had to release the drogue target and its thousand-yard cable on the airfield prior to landing, since the pilot could not land towing this appendage. Released drogues sometimes caused damage when they hit the ground. The previously-mentioned damage to a BAT Flight Oxford from a drogue released from a Lysander at Docking was a case in point.

No 288 Squadron, which was based at RAF Digby in Lincolnshire, frequently kept Martinet aircraft at Docking to provide towing facilities for gunnery practice. Docking and Bircham Newton squadrons flying offensive operations would also have to attend an armament practice camp (APC) for

bombing practice. A tragic accident happened in June 1942, when a Hudson belonging to 407 Squadron crashed during a 9-day APC at RAF Thorney Island. The aircraft hit the mast of a wrecked ship that was being used for bombing practice. It crashed into the sea and caught fire, killing the Canadian crew and an instructor from the APC. Two of the victims of this accident are buried at the local war graves cemetery in Great Bircham churchyard.

Warwick Training Unit

By 1943, Bircham Newton was playing a major role in Coastal Commands ASR operations and evaluating the Warwick bomber's suitability as a Hudson replacement in this role. The Warwick was not terribly successful as a torpedo bomber, but it gradually replaced the Hudson and Anson aircraft on ASR duties, carrying Lindholme rescue gear and also an airborne lifeboat. Consequently the Command's first Warwick ASR Mk Is started to appear at Bircham and Docking in the summer of 1943. The Warwick Training Unit was formed at Docking in June 1943 to train Coastal Command pilots on this new aircraft and to conduct trials dropping the Mk I airborne lifeboat. The unit was to train 20 long-range air-sea rescue crews on the Warwick. On completion the crews were to ferry their own aircraft overseas. The unit was allocated 5 Wellingtons for conversion ferrying and 20 ASR Warwicks for advanced training. Training courses were scheduled to cover one month commencing 25 June. The Unit moved to Bircham Newton early in the following month leaving behind a Ferry Training Flight at Docking. This Flight trained crews to deliver Warwicks to overseas ASR squadrons. One of the Warwick aircraft was destroyed at Docking on 13 August 1943, when it caught fire on the ground.

The fully developed version of the Warwick ASR aircraft could carry the heavier Mk II lifeboat, which was more than 9 m long and could carry ten survivors. The Warwick ASR MK I contributed a great deal to the air-sea rescue services and served with fourteen squadrons. The Warwick Training Unit became the Air Sea Rescue ASR Training Unit at the beginning of October 1943 and moved on to Thornaby in the following month.

No. 1693 ASR Training Unit

Air-sea rescue training for Coastal Command aircrews was briefly conducted at Docking (using Wellington III and Warwick ASR Mk I aircraft) when No 1693 ASR Training Unit relocated to Docking for the period May-July 1945. This was one of the final units to use the airfield.

6. Life at Docking during World War 2

'They touched down half way along the runway, expecting a much larger airfield. Consequently, most of them crashed through the hedge at the end of the runway and ended up in a ploughed field.'

Members of the Women's Auxiliary Air Force (WAAF) were employed at RAF Docking as clerks, mess stewards, cooks, MT drivers and on operational duties. They made their own unique contributions to RAF Docking and have many stories to tell. Mrs Ellen Finch, who now lives at the nearby village of Stanhoe, served on the camp between 1941 and 1943. Ellen, who had originally trained as a parachute packer, worked as a mess steward at the officers' mess, where she was a barmaid. She said that at one point she lived at Bircham Newton and cycled more than four miles to work at RAF Docking. However, like most of the WAAF girls that worked at Docking, she was later billeted in Docking Hall. She recalled that all of the airmen and airwomen working at the remote sites were issued with RAF bicycles, which kept them all fit.

'One morning near the railway station at Docking I had to cycle past a crashed plane that was armed with a live torpedo. I have never cycled so fast in my life...Unfortunately, plane crashes were a quite a common occurrence...We were warned about imminent air raids or forced landings of aircraft with bombs on board, so that we could get as far away as possible. I used to run across the fields towards Lugden Hill Farm.'

Docking Railway Station

59

Ellen remembered the visiting Canadians, Poles, and Americans who flew from Docking.

> 'They had plenty of rowdy parties when they were not flying. However, they were not allowed to drink if they were flying on operations the following morning...I was very saddened at the huge loss of life amongst the aircrew. They were incredibly brave young men, not much older than boys...The most difficult job that I was ever given was to pack up the personal belongings of deceased airmen, so that they could be returned to their families.'

Ellen married in 1943 and was relieved to escape from this distressing work.

Another ex-Docking WAAF is Mrs Doris Driver, who now lives at Great Massingham in Norfolk. Doris, née Rix, was born in Docking's neighbouring village of Sedgeford. After joining the WAAF, she was kitted out in Gloucester, and did her 'square bashing' on the sea front at Morecambe, before getting her first posting to Bircham Newton quite close to her home village. However, she had been recruited as a Clerk Special Duties, for which there was no opening at Bircham, and consequently found herself sweeping the barrack room floors. Happily it wasn't long before her services were required in the Flying Control Section at Docking. Doris recalled that when she first arrived at Docking, flying control functions were being conducted from a temporary hut on the airfield, while the new control tower was being built nearby; they moved into the control tower soon after she arrived, towards the end of 1942. The temporary control tower was then used by BAT Flight.

Initially Doris was billeted in Docking Hall, the ancestral home of the Hare family. Mrs J. H. M. Hare occupied the lower floors and she was in the attic. She was transported to work in a lorry, which used to call at the Hall to pick up the WAAF girls. Later she moved into a WAAF hut, much closer to the airfield.

> 'This hut was so new, that they hadn't even laid any paths. There was mud and puddles everywhere...Consequently, we had to "slosh" from place to place in our gumboots.'

Before she was issued with a bicycle, Doris used to walk into Docking on her off duty periods.

> 'I can recall purchasing delicious buns from Mr T.R. Wagg, who had a small shop in the front room of his cottage near to the bakery.'

Doris loved RAF Docking because of its relaxed atmosphere.

> 'Nobody was rank conscious, and everyone was on first name terms...On a shift in the control tower there would be eight WAAF girls, comprising four R/T operators and four special duties clerks. The

R/T operators would be in contact with aircraft, talking to the aircrew particularly as they prepared for take-offs and landings, while the clerks would keep the movement boards up to date, recording all messages, take-offs, landings and the like. They would also plot the position of any aircraft that had ditched in the sea...Special duties clerks were the 'dogs bodies', who would do any administrative duties required during the shift...Girls that were on special duties weren't always popular with their colleagues, because they were excused all parades...Of course, this didn't include pay parades.'

Doris recalled that there were searchlight batteries at Docking, connected via landlines to the control tower.

'There were even army gunners based there to defend the airfield'

Doris sometimes visited Bircham Newton's control tower and underground Ops Room on relief duties.

'WAAF girls had to wear trousers in the Ops Room, because it distracted the men if they climbed ladders to reach the various display boards in skirts...Even visiting aircrew that landed at Docking would be ferried to Bircham for supper and for debriefing in the Ops Room...I can vividly remember one navigator, who I think was from North Coates, asking me to look after his Mae West life jacket while he attended the debriefing at Bircham. When he returned and collected it again prior to takeoff, he was so grateful that he promised to give me half his chocolate ration on his next visit to our control tower... Unfortunately, he was killed shortly afterwards when his aircraft crashed just after take off.'

Doris had fond memories of 320 (Dutch) Squadron personnel, who were billeted at Bircham but flew their night operations from Docking.

'They had plenty of parties and were always very friendly to all the Docking ground staff, generously sharing their chocolate rations.'

However, American aircrew did not impress her as much.

'I can remember seeing several B17 aircraft crash land at Docking one Saturday afternoon. They touched down half way along the runway, expecting a much larger airfield. Consequently, most of them crashed through the hedge at the end of the runway and ended up in a ploughed field....After that, I was suspicious of all American pilots.'

61

Doris did fly herself at Docking, as a passenger in an Airspeed Oxford of the BAT Flight and found it a thrilling experience. Another aircraft type that she remembered clearly was the air-sea rescue Hudson carrying the airborne lifeboat. 'The life-boat made the aircraft look pregnant,' she remarked.

Doris Rix, (on the left) enjoying herself in Docking in 1943

An ex-WAAF who served at Docking as a friend of Doris Rix is Mrs Dorothy Jackson, who now lives at Finedon in Northamptonshire. Dorothy recalls that it was possible to obtain a rare luxury in the form of a free bar of chocolate from the Salvation Army, who occupied a wooden hut situated near to the Oddfellows Hall in Docking.

'We would walk or cycle to Docking from the RAF camp to collect this treat...Despite the exercise, it did nothing for our waistlines.'

The hut in question had a long and interesting history. It started life as an isolation hospital near RAF Bircham Newton, but was moved to Docking during WW2 to be used as a British Restaurant. These restaurants (or canteens) were set up all over the country to provide cheap wholesome food during the days of strict rationing. It was probably the only place in Docking where the airmen and airwomen could dine out in wartime. From all accounts, the meals were very cheap (between 2 shillings and half-a-crown per meal) but very basic and rather boring. The contemporary local newspapers mention a services canteen, which was opened at Docking in 1942 as a private concern, sponsored by Mrs J.H. Hare. By 1943 this was being run by the YMCA, with Docking ladies as voluntary helpers. It is assumed that this was the same establishment. In more recent times, the hut was acquired by the Women's Institute, which held all its meetings there for many years. The locals could hire the hut from the W.I. to hold functions, such as birthday parties and wedding receptions. Sadly, the hut was closed in 1998.

A recent picture of the hut used as Docking's British Restaurant in WW2

The nearby Oddfellows Hall, now called the Dr W.E. Ripper Memorial Hall, was regularly used to hold dances during the war years; it was nicknamed the 'Dustbin', although neither of the two friends could remember the origin of this name. Dorothy recalled,

> 'We had a very obliging chemist in the village who kept his supply of Yardley's cosmetics under the counter for us.'

This was a rare treat in times when most young ladies had to make their own make up and use gravy browning and pencil-drawn seams for silk stockings. Like many of the girls serving at Docking, Dorothy was billeted in Docking Hall for a time, and was soon issued with her RAF bicycle.

'It was like being at a boarding school as there were several beds to a room and we sat at long tables in the dining room...The second night that I had my bicycle we went to the local pub at Brancaster to celebrate, and on the way back I was summonsed by the local bobby for riding without a light! The upshot of this was that the actual summons wasn't sent to me at the camp, but was sent to my home address. As my father was a policeman, you can imagine what a 'talking to' I received on my next home leave...If we wanted to go into the local seaside resort of Hunstanton, we had to hitch-hike, which never seemed risky in those days...One day one of our mob had a date in Hunstanton and decided to hitch-hike. The only vehicle that passed her was one that she described as "Dan, Dan the Sani-Can Man". As you can imagine, she refused to accept a lift from this smelly contraption and ended up walking the whole eight miles to keep her appointment. By the time she arrived, her young man had left, thinking that he had been stood up. Despite this disappointment, our friend had a good laugh when she told us about it later.'

63

Dorothy (seated second from left) attending a birthday party in Docking Hall

When she left Docking, Dorothy was posted to Coastal Command Headquarters at Chatham. 'My time at Chatham was interesting but not nearly as nice as being at Docking,' she remarked.

Mr John Lucas, from Deal in Kent, was a Leading Aircraftsman serving at Docking during 1944 and 1945. He worked in the Flying Control Section as part of a radio control unit that was housed in the ground floor of the control tower. His task, which he performed with a WAAF colleague, was to maintain communications with aircraft using radio (R/T), relaying messages and providing assistance to them as they approached the airfield to land.

> 'The flares along the flarepath had to be lit by hand at night. This meant that we often had to delay incoming aircraft while this task was performed.'

John also acted as a driver for the Motor Transport (MT) Section. He frequently drove the ambulance used to ferry seriously injured personnel from Docking to Bircham Newton. Docking had small sick quarters and some medical personnel, but serious casualties had to be rushed to the parent station for assessment and treatment by the medical officer.

> 'The ambulance and a fire truck were usually parked quite close to the control tower, so that we could quickly respond to any 'prangs' on the airfield...When such an event happened, I would sprint to the ambulance and drive it to the scene of the accident.'

The most horrific event that John witnessed was the crash of Squadron Leader R.L.J. Fitch, which occurred in May 1945. The Squadron Leader, who served with No. 2 Armament Practice Camp (APC), flew his aircraft into farm cottages that were situated at the southern edge of the airfield, close to the Docking to Burnham Market road and the adjacent railway line.

> 'I can remember the officer circling around the airfield in an erratic manner, before he plunged his aircraft into the cottages in an apparent act of suicide brought on by marital problems...I drove the ambulance over to the crash site, where we found a scene of devastation. I was the actual person who eventually found the Squadron Leader's body amongst the rubble and twisted metal. We later recovered it and drove it to the morgue at Bircham Newton. I have a vivid memory of this terrible incident, which still disturbs me today. One of my lasting memories is of the passing trains, which slowed down to enable the driver and passengers to view the scene. It was the gawping passengers that upset me the most.'

John also recalled crash landings made by aircraft returning damaged or short of fuel from operational missions. A Lancaster bomber that was suffering from engine trouble performed one such crash landing.

'I witnessed it making a very heavy landing, which destroyed the undercarriage. One of the wheels, probably the tail wheel, bounced across the grass airfield narrowly missing the control tower where I was working.'

Although most of Docking's operational flying had ceased by 1945, beam approach training and target-towing continued.

'They seemed to be flying around the airfield continuously doing "circuits and bumps"...
The drogues would be released prior to landing and would often be seen fluttering to the ground.'

**A Lysander flying
over Docking church**

John's most cherished memories of Docking are of courting his future wife, who also served there as WAAF in the post office. They would attend dances at the village hall to the musical accompaniment of a local RAF dance band. Other pleasures included drinking in the local pubs and cycling to Brancaster on their RAF issue bicycles.

Many air raids were conducted against Docking airfield during the war, and some bombs fell on the village. The intensity of these attacks, may be illustrated from the raids in 1940 and 1941.

On 5 September 1940, approximately eight incendiary bombs were dropped around the airfield, but there were no casualties. A week later, on 12 September, Norwich Observer Corps reported that enemy aircraft were trailing a Hudson aircraft that had flown overhead. Shortly afterwards incendiary bombs dropped all around the airfield, but mostly along the railway lines. Most of the fires were quickly extinguished, except for two significant fires close to Docking railway station. Three days later, on 15 September, two heavy bombs were dropped west of the neighbouring village of Sedgeford, followed by two more towards the small hamlet of Fring. To complete a bad month, bombs were dropped to the north of the airfield on 19 September. One bomb caused a crater 20 ft across and 8 ft deep in a nearby field, while a second was determined to be an oil bomb. On 20 October, an enemy aircraft dropped a landmine, which descended by parachute near the airfield flarepath. Fortunately a naval party was able to destroy the mine before it could cause further damage. Four days later, on the 24th, an enemy fighter attacked a Blenheim aircraft from No. 17 Operational Training Unit, which was on a training flight over the airfield. As a result, the Blenheim's hydraulic system and port petrol tank was severely damaged and the aircraft was set on fire. It subsequently crashed on the airfield but the crew survived.

On 6 January 1941, an enemy aircraft, believed to be a Dornier, conducted bomb and machine-gun attacks on Docking village. The civil police reported that the enemy aircraft dropped eight bombs near Burntstork cottages on the Sedgeford Road and brought down the grid cable. Hall Farm was also machine-gunned, but there were no casualties. A few days later, on 11 March, an enemy aircraft dropped 200–300 incendiaries across the airfield, although no serious damage was done. A small fire ignited in farm buildings at the rear of the landing ground, but this was quickly extinguished.

Perhaps the most devastating raid of the war occurred just before midnight on 16 May 1941, when Sunderland farmhouse and a collocated granary were bombed and destroyed with several casualties. The farmhouse was being used as sleeping quarters at the time. Apparently this raid happened just after one or more Docking aircraft had landed from an operational mission. So it is thought that the enemy aircraft followed the returning RAF aircraft to the airfield with disastrous results.

A description of the farmhouse bombing is contained in the Operations Record Book (ORB) for Bircham Newton (AIR 28/73):

2302:   'Purple' warning received
2330:   Burst of bombs heard from Ops. Room.

	Docking report that a heavy bomb had burst on the far side of the aerodrome
2340:	'Red' warning received
2345:	Docking report that the farmhouse has been hit and crew's sleeping quarters demolished. Ambulance and M.O.s sent out.

Casualties: 3 airmen killed and 15 wounded, most of them seriously

Further evidence that the enemy followed returning aircraft was provided on 7 July, when a Blenheim of 500 Squadron was shot down as it was landing at the airfield. The entire crew was killed in this incident. On 13 August, bombs were again dropped on the airfield, shortly after a warning was received from Bircham Newton to extinguish the Docking flarepath. However, no report is available as to the extent of the damage on this occasion. In the following month, on 29 September, bombs and incendiaries were dropped on the airfield causing ten craters but no casualties.

The aircrews of visiting squadrons provided contrasting views of RAF Docking. No. 811 Squadron of the Fleet Air Arm, on loan to Coastal Command, flew night operations from Docking using its Swordfish aircraft from August to December 1942. The Squadron was employed laying mines off the Dutch coast or in the approaches to enemy-occupied harbours. It also attacked enemy shipping convoys using torpedoes. Although the aircrews were comfortably billeted at Bircham Newton, they spent most evenings on standby at Docking, waiting around until the small hours, in their flying suits, ready to scramble within fifteen minutes of a suitable target being assigned to them. Sometimes, they would get a change of scene when they flew off at dusk to an alternative airfield so that they could attack targets that were out of range from Docking. The author of the book *Bring Back My Stringbag*, one of 811 Squadron's wartime pilots, described Docking as 'a windy little airfield without proper runways, possessing draughty tents and rickety tables with no facilities beyond cups of cocoa and sandwiches.'

The second squadron, not subject to fifteen-minute standby restrictions, was more complimentary. No. 304 (Polish) Squadron was relocated to Docking in April 1943 to be re-equipped with Wellington Mk X aircraft and to be retrained as a torpedo bomber squadron. (See page 00) During their stay at Docking the Squadron personnel were billeted in barrack huts beside the Docking-Brancaster road. They described their accommodation as being comfortable and Docking's mess food as being excellent, which they thought most unusual for a Coastal Command station.

An ex-member of 521 Squadron, Mr Jack Allaway (see page 00), who recovered from serious burns following a crash at Docking in October 1943, has fond memories of Docking. Jack was called up when he was eighteen and volunteered to train in the RAF. He subsequently became a navigator after aircrew training in Ireland. He joined No. 521 Squadron and flew several meteorological reconnaissance missions in Hampden aircraft from Docking prior to his crash, which ended his flying days. Although he couldn't remember much about the layout of the camp, Jack remembered being billeted in a Nissen hut quite close to the road from Docking to Brancaster. He also recalled that 521 Squadron had a remote dispersal equipped with Blister hangars and tents. He could also remember participating in air-sea rescue training, using dinghies on Heacham beach.

Jack didn't expect to survive the war. He realized that flying met. operations was a dangerous business, and he had known of several airmen that had perished during his brief time in the service.

'I wasn't frightened though; it was more a case of being resigned to my situation and most likely fate. I decided to take on a positive attitude, trying to enjoy life on every occasion that I could...I used my RAF bicycle to visit Docking village and other local attractions, such as the royal Sandringham estate. I also loved to play tennis at Bircham Newton with my Canadian skipper Jack Maxwell.'

Jack also recalled drinking in the local pubs, attending dances in Docking village hall and nights out in the local towns, such as King's Lynn.

Les Hart, a pilot from 519 Squadron, engaged in Rhombus flights with Docking's 521 Squadron (see page 00), recalled that Rhombus crews were debriefed when they arrived at Docking and were then provided with a meal, invariably eggs, bacon and chips with bread, butter, marmalade and tea. They then retired to a Nissen hut kept especially for the visiting crew and sank into bed. After resting, they usually had the rest of the day to themselves, since they didn't fly their reverse trip to Skitten, near Wick, until the following day. The crew would borrow bicycles from 521 Squadron and cycle into the village for a pint in one of Docking's pubs. Les remembered there was a baker's shop opposite one of the pubs, where they could purchase delicious meat pies. Later they would cycle back to camp, often four to a bike. To take the short cut back to their Nissen hut they had to negotiate a tricky hole in the hedge. After a few beers, this was usually too tight a squeeze for their overloaded bike and they invariably ended up on the ground or sprawled all over the hedge. As pilot and captain, he usually had to take the blame.

Les was the unfortunate pilot responsible for the crash landing of a Ventura aircraft on his first flight to Docking on 29 April 1944. In his own words:

'The day in question found me flying the Rhombus, landing at Docking, Norfolk. It was an early take-off, ten past six and although only four and a half hours duration, we were buffeted about in cloud and flying blind for two hours. We emerged from the cloud near the coast, made a good landfall, and soon found the airfield. I executed the mandatory left hand circuit of the airfield, looked at the ground signals, checked wind speed and direction and noted the airfield boundaries. It appeared as a very large field without runways, and having what seemed to be a path worn in the grass crossing it about midway. I imagined that a path had been worn by airmen crossing to dispersals on foot or bicycle. I subsequently wished that I had paid more attention to that feature.

With so much room for landing, I made a high approach, aiming to touch down ahead of the path, which lay at right angles to my line of descent. I decided to 'wheel her in' – meaning touching down on the main two undercarriage wheels only, and with the tail up, rather than the normal 'three pointer' (touching down on main and tail wheels simultaneously). My reason was to avoid the tendency of the Ventura (and Hudson) to swing on touchdown, i.e. veer off violently to one side, usually port, and possibly groundloop. It required a slightly higher landing speed.

She touched down smoothly at around 90 knots in the tail up position. Suddenly there was an almighty crunch as the main undercarriage was ripped away and the aircraft crashed down on its belly, bending the propellers back along the engine cowlings. Seconds later as we slithered along came another crunch and the aircraft cartwheeled to the left, fortunately keeping on its belly.

Two aspects of the construction of Venturas and Hudsons made it more than normally essential to distance oneself speedily from a crash: their petrol tanks were not tanks at all but simply sealed sections of the wing cavities which a very heavy landing could fracture; and the high magnesium content of their metal, which caused them to burn particularly fiercely. For these reasons crews who flew them wasted no time escaping to a safe distance after a prang. This occasion was no exception for the navigator and WOp/AGs but my own behaviour afterwards seemed rather odd. I remember pulling the overhead escape hatch lever before we came to a halt and the hatch flying off.

I was vaguely aware of crew members shouting as they clambered over me to heave themselves through the roof opening. Possibly the sudden violent and totally unexpected crash had dazed me until I heard the crew outside shouting to me to get out. They had seen while using me as a ladder that I was unhurt, but I felt no sense of urgency. Apart from the shouting, all was peace and quiet after the crunching and tearing of metal. There were no flames and I was quite relaxed as I hoisted myself out.

By this time the ambulance and fire engine had arrived and were relieved to find nothing more serious than bruising, and that the aircraft did not burn. I had recovered sufficiently from the shock to try to establish the cause of the debacle. It transpired that the 'path' was in fact a ditch, which formed the boundary of the airfield. Still travelling at about 80 knots when we hit it, it is not surprising that it robbed us of the undercart. The second impact was with a 'totem pole' – a tall pole erected just beyond a grass airfield boundary when the airfield has a hump in the middle. It has shrouded lights near the top which face a pilot taking off, providing him with a point to line up on and keep straight during take-off runs in darkness or poor visibility. We had struck the pole on the wing between the fuselage and the port engine, demolishing the pole, taking a large bite out of the wing, and causing us to cartwheel. Realising that I was entirely to blame, my heart sank. The members of the crew were supportive despite having such a narrow squeak, and did their best to cheer me up – emphasizing that we had walked away from it and that was the important thing.

I received short shrift from the CO of the resident 521 Squadron who, having taken a written statement from me, tore me off a gigantic strip for messing up his airfield. He telephoned my own CO to report my handiwork, provided a railway warrant for the four of us to return to Wick by train, and suggested that the sooner we left the premises the better.'

The 519 Squadron Operations Record Book for that day was very succinct:

29.4.44   0610   Rhombus Met. Sortie in Ventura 'H' Overshot on landing at Docking at 1032 hrs

Les was to face the wrath of his CO when he arrived back at his home station, and the subsequent Board of Enquiry found him guilty of gross carelessness, leading to a red-ink endorsement in his logbook. However, with his pride dented, he soon returned to operational flying. In 1945 Les joined 521 Squadron, which had moved to Langham from Docking in October 1944, to begin conversion to Fortress II aircraft.

Two local men who knew the wartime airfield well were Alan Watts and Tony Arter, who both still live in Docking village. On behalf of his employer, Mr B. Playford, Alan delivered the morning newspapers to the various messes and clubs around the RAF camp, assisted by Tony. Consequently both young men spent quite a lot of time at the various RAF sites. They vividly remember several spectacular aircraft crashes around Docking, including the Hampden belonging to the Canadian 415 (Swordfish) Squadron that crashed, armed with a live torpedo, near to Docking railway station in 1943. Alan lived in one of the council houses along Brancaster road at the time, quite close to where the aircraft came down.

'I remember that we were all evacuated from our houses and led across the railway lines to a safe area while the aircraft was disarmed.'

Both men can remember watching several American B-17 aircraft crash landing on Docking airfield. Alan recalls,

'I heard that the American aircraft were on a bombing mission when they experienced serious icing problems and had to abort. So, fully armed and bombed up, they attempted to make emergency landings at Docking...'

Tony added,

'Most of them "belly flopped" onto the runway making a terrible mess and causing lots of damage.'

Alan remembered the night that the farmhouse was bombed in 1941. It happened early in the morning, several hours before he arrived at the camp.

'Many thought that the German pilots had followed RAF aircraft that were returning from an operation across the North Sea and had consequently been led to Docking...I think that there were fourteen victims, including some that lost their lives. I'm sure that some WAAF's were among the casualties.'

On a lighter note, Alan remembered a humorous incident that happened when he parked his trade bicycle inside a hangar used by the BAT Flight.

'When I returned for it, the airmen had painted KILLER on my bike using blue doping paint. Thereafter I was known as "Killer" Watts, which was obviously meant to rhyme with Kilo Watts.'

The aircrew would often take Alan up for unofficial flights in their aircraft, when they were performing local training sorties. He was an air cadet, who was allowed the occasional air experience flight, providing it was properly authorized.

'I would usually take my cadet uniform with me on the off chance of obtaining a flight...The aircrew would sign my "chit" and strap me into a large sit-on parachute, and before I realized what was happening, they would push me into an aircraft and they would start taxiing for take off... I flew in lots of different aircraft types at Docking, including the Oxfords from BAT Flight.'

Mr Derek Rolfe, who now lives in Canada, was also an ATC cadet in wartime Docking. In 1940, Derek's father, Police Sergeant A.E. Rolfe, was posted to Docking and Derek spent the war years as a young man in the village. After eaving school, he worked for Mr Fred Curry, who was an undertaker, builder and decorator in the village. His initial wage was five shillings a week. Mr Curry had the undertaking contract with Bircham Newton, so they were kept very busy coping with the many air-crash fatalities that occurred. When they were doing building work Derek was the general 'gofer'. He was frequently asked to go back to the workshop to get bags of cement, ladders, timber and the like. This meant cycling back to the Mr Curry's workshop near the Oddfellows Hall and then walking back to the site with the requested items tied to his overloaded bicycle. His bicycle was his most prized possession.

ATC cadet Derek Rolfe, aged 14, in 1943

'After all, if you didn't have a bike you would be stuck in the village. Our machines were made up from parts coming from all kinds of models, but they all flew. We all became Spitfire pilots, racing around the village at break-neck speeds. Many crashes happened, and skinned knees and elbows were the norm. Summer was the busiest time for our bikes, which were often used for trips to Brancaster beach. We would be dressed in just our swimming trunks, carrying our towels under the seat. Often we would ride straight into the sea without stopping, we were so hot after the ride from Docking. We would also use our bikes to get to ATC parades. The ATC Flight HQ was situated in a small school room in the village of Snettisham. Quite a lot of us boys from Docking would attend. We would set out on our bikes for Snettisham come rain or shine, and would get up one heck of a speed going down the hill to Fring, only to slow right down on the other side. I remember that my father would teach us Morse code on a piece of equipment made from an old gramophone and a six volt battery.'

To arrange for air experience flights, Derek made contact with pilots, mostly Canadian members of No. 415 Squadron, at the Hare Inn, which was run by his aunt Edna Jacobs.

'All we had to do was put on our ATC uniforms and turn up at the dispersals, turning left at the control tower. There were Wellingtons, Venturas, Oxfords and Hudsons. Oh, if only I had kept a log book.'

73

Since my contacts were mostly with Canadian pilots, most of my flying was done in Wellingtons, performing non-operational flights, ranging from 20 minutes to more than 2 hours in length. You always knew when a short flight was coming up, because you would see a LAC or a corporal climb aboard. This would indicate a radio check or some other small adjustment while in flight. The flights I enjoyed the most were practice bombing runs with smoke bombs on a floating target somewhere out in the Wash. Gunnery practice was also carried out at the same time. A good place to sit was in the blister on the top of the fuselage. One had to remember to hold on tight, for on a rough day one could get a nasty bump on the head. I remember one flight very well to this day. We left Docking and climbed to about three thousand feet until we were over Ringstead. Then we started a gradual descent down to roof-top height by the time we arrived over Hunstanton. Then we flew down the Green and out over the pier. As we left the pier behind us, we descended until we were quite close to the water, maintaining this altitude for quite some time, lifting the aircraft only to bank.

I had a couple of rides in Oxfords, from the BAT Flight. One had to sit between the two pilots on the spare seat. On both flights I was given a helmet with a headset, so that I could listen to what was going on. On one of the flights, I remember seeing Ely Cathedral on the outbound leg. We never took in the chances we were taking. In later years I have often thought to myself, what if a German fighter had come along and taken a shot at us? I don't think we would have had much chance of survival really.'

Another local man, Mr Colin Coe, who lives at Lower Farm near to the former RAF camp at Bircham Newton, also remembers RAF Docking during the war years. As a young boy he sometimes accompanied his father, Mr Clifford Coe, when he delivered milk to the RAF stations at Bircham and Docking.

'We delivered milk to the "Cookhouse" at Docking, which was situated about a mile outside the village along the Brancaster road. On one occasion I spotted a large tray of cold sausages, which I presume had been prepared for the breakfast meal. I was sure that they wouldn't miss one sausage so I helped myself, devouring it quickly before anyone noticed. Luckily nobody caught me in the act, or I would have been in big trouble, particularly from my father...One of my most poignant memories was to find several full milk bottles when we collected the empties. We always knew that this meant that several airmen had failed to return from the operational missions conducted over the previous evening.'

74

Colin's parents accommodated lodgers from the RAF camp during the war years. At one time they had some of Bircham Newton's weather forecasters living with them.

'This meant that we always had up-to-date weather forecasts, much better than those available in the newspapers or broadcast on the radio. My father even stopped looking at his piece of seaweed that was hanging up outside the back door. I vaguely remember another wartime guest, who flew operational missions and had survived two "ditchings" in the North Sea.'

Some bombs fell on Bircham village during the war, destroying the local mill, and Colin's home at Lower Farm suffered a near miss when bombs exploded in a nearby field. Once, when he was walking home from school with some friends, a Dornier passed overhead, flying so low that they waved to the pilot, who surprised them by waving back.

'We were quite relieved when our new friend avoided the anti-aircraft guns defending Bircham Newton airfield. The gunners must have been asleep.'

Mrs Doris Rumbellow, (née Coates), who now lives in the nearby village of Heacham, also remembers Docking in the 1940s. Prior to her marriage in 1949, Doris lived in a cottage on Lugden Hill Farm, quite close to the wartime airfield. She remembers the noise of the aircraft as they flew in and out of the airfield and bombs exploding in a field quite close to Lugden Hill farmhouse. Unlike nearby Sunderland Farm, Lugden Hill Farm was not requisitioned for the RAF and remained as a working farm throughout the war. However, opposite to the entrance to the farm, on top of Lugden Hill, there was a hutted RAF site, which she thought was occupied by Canadian airmen at one time. Doris's mother did their washing for them.

Doris regularly walked to work at Docking along the Brancaster road past the various hutted RAF sites. However, the sites were guarded and placed out of bounds to local civilians. After leaving school Doris worked for two of Docking's largest employers T.R. Wagg the local baker and C.W. Masters Ltd, a specialist seed merchant. There was a large fire at C.W. Masters premises in 1943, which destroyed the original seed store. The modern buildings, locally known as 'the Granaries', were rebuilt after this fire and extended in the 1950s.

Robert Perowne, of High House Farm, remembers his late grandfather, Mr William H.C. Peacock, who was the farmer at Sunderland Farm during WW2, telling him about the crops that had been damaged or destroyed by aircraft crashes and their resultant fires. His grandfather rarely received adequate compensation for such 'acts of war'. Robert works the same land around Sunderland Farm today.

'Although I don't often plough up aircraft parts, I frequently trawl up wires and fittings that belonged to the old airfield lighting.'

In his wartime diaries, Bill Davis, a wireless operator/air gunner on No. 521 Squadron, provides great insight into the tension and fear experienced by aircrew who were flying regular met operations exposed to enemy aircraft and flak from enemy convoys and ground batteries. Bill flew several dangerous PAMPA sorties into enemy territory as a re-trained navigator aboard Mosquito aircraft. He was often quite ill with a bad stomach, probably due to the stress of flying. However, he wouldn't use his medical problems as an excuse to get away from his flying duties since, in his own words, 'it would be too cowardly'. Bill's diary also illustrates the boredom of waiting for operations and the extreme discomfort of the cold when flying at high altitude. His way of escape, shared by many of his colleagues, seems to have been sleeping whenever possible, gambling at cards and regular heavy drinking sessions in the evenings, when not on early flying duties the next morning. They also loved getting around the piano in the mess to sing dirty songs. He describes nights dancing and drinking in King's Lynn (The Globe) and Hunstanton (The KitCat). Dances were also held in the RAF mess, but Bill was often sickened by the drunkenness. He was particularly disgusted at seeing WAAFs drinking pints and 'making themselves cheap'. At such social gatherings, there seems to have been some resentment of the Canadians from 407 Squadron, who were paid much more than their RAF counterparts, and were consequently very popular with the local women. Quieter evenings were often spent in local pubs, within walking distance of Bircham Newton. One of Bill's favourite drinking haunts was the Norfolk Hero pub at Stanhoe. Bill often biked from Bircham to the swimming baths at Hunstanton, and later, when he lived with his wife and children at Heacham, he would bike to and from work, a round trip of 18 miles.

During his initial tour of duty in Norfolk with 521 Squadron, Bill was billeted at Bircham Newton, which played a larger part in his story than the satellite at Docking. However, he describes take-offs and landings that were made from Docking during January/February 1942, when Bircham airfield was closed because of deep snow. He recalls seeing about 300 airmen tramping down the snow at Bircham, in an attempt to make a serviceable runway.

To escape from the stress of operations and the confines of the RAF camp, many of the airmen socialized with the local people in the public houses. One favourite haunt was the Railway Inn, the closest hostelry to most of the RAF accommodation along the road out of Docking leading to Brancaster. As its name implies, the Railway Inn was very close to the railway station, the airmen's gateway to the outside world.

Generally, airmen posted to Docking or Bircham Newton came by train, arriving at Docking railway station. Trains would also provide escape to other local towns or leave destinations. One could not arrive or depart without confronting the Railway Inn. It was a popular place for the airmen to stop and refresh themselves after a long railway journey. For many of them it became the local, where they drank, played darts, sang and met the local girls. Many of them stumbled back along the Brancaster road towards their barracks much the worst for wear. The unfortunate ones would not be seen in the pub again because they were shot down the next day.

Docking railway station was on a branch line that ran between King's Lynn and Wells, although it was necessary to change at Heacham, which was on the King's Lynn to Hunstanton line. Many airmen who had enjoyed a good night out in King's Lynn would forget to change trains at Heacham and travel on to Hunstanton. They would then have to walk home to Docking, a distance of about eight miles. One unfortunate airman who made this mistake and then tried to re-use his out-dated King's Lynn to Docking railway ticket, which had not been taken from him at Hunstanton, was summoned to appear before the magistrates in King's Lynn for attempting to travel without having paid his fare. He explained to the magistrate that he had kept this old ticket because he had not completed the original journey from King's Lynn to Docking, and therefore felt justified in presenting it to the ticket collector on a subsequent occasion. Unfortunately, the magistrate was not impressed and issued the airman with a stiff fine.

The late Ted Beales, one of Docking's best-known wartime policemen recalled in an interview with a local newspaper in 1992 that there were often fights between servicemen outside the Docking pubs. They were usually started by arguments, but often ended amicably with one combatant buying the other a drink. Ted also recalled that at the Norfolk Hero in Stan-hoe, they would sell the airmen beer by the pail. A group of them would club together and buy a pail of beer, which they would consume through the evening by dipping their glasses in the pail.

Ted began his Docking service in 1939 when he joined the Norfolk Constabulary War Reserve. Initially he lived at North Creake, six and a half miles from Docking, and would

PC Ted Beales, one of Docking's wartime policemen

77

cycle to and from work, returning during the hours of darkness. Cycling at night was difficult because he had to have a reflector or hood over his cycle lamp to minimize the light that could be seen from the air. Car drivers couldn't see him too well either because of headlamp masks required on motor vehicles. When the war was over, Ted transferred to the police force, serving for 28 years in Docking, where he was affectionately known as 'Dixon of Docking' or 'Beales on Wheels', because he always performed his duties on a bicycle.

Ex-pilot Frank Goff thought that the practice of serving beer in a pail had started during his first tour of duty at Bircham Newton in 1941, when he served with 206 Squadron. The Hero was a favourite drinking place for squadron personnel at that time. He recalled that the beer was kept in wooden barrels in a kind of outdoor lean-to, which kept it nice and cool. However, it took an age for the landlord to pour each pint from a wooden barrel, so the airmen borrowed a NAAFI pail, which they took to the pub for the landlord to fill while they were enjoying their first drinks. After a time, they marked the pail with the squadron's number and left it at the pub for use on subsequent visits.

The Norfolk Hero was also a favourite haunt of 521 Squadron, the Met. Squadron. In his diaries, Bill Davis describes one party when the Squadron bought all of the beer available in the pub for a private party, hanging a 'no beer' sign on the door to discourage everyone else. Beer was served in buckets as usual, and twelve squadron members consumed approximately 144 pints of it. When they had consumed all the beer, two of them were sent to the next pub in the village to obtain two more pails full. Bill recalled that everyone finished up very 'tight' and had a grand times singing to their hearts' content. Their only regret was that they had to be up early for an operational trip. Unfortunately, the Norfolk Hero Inn, also previously known as the Nelson and as the Hero, closed in 1964 and is now a private dwelling.

Another off-duty occupation very prevalent in those wartime days of meat shortages was the poaching of rabbits and game. Apart from feeding their families, it is likely that the local poachers could supplement their wages by selling their ill-gotten gains to one of the local butchers 'Lou' Bayfield or 'Crew' Masters. Ted Beales admitted that he turned a blind eye and didn't attempt to catch many poachers, since he knew they were mostly just trying to feed their families in a time of meat rationing and great shortages. Talking to a local newspaper about the war years, Ted said,

'Really all the trouble we had then was punch ups outside pubs and the odd fellow poaching. But then times were hard and people had to poach to get by.'

Life for the locals in Docking was very austere during the war years. Most things were in short supply. Rationing began at the outbreak of war in 1939 and covered such commodities as petrol, food and clothing. It is the food rationing that is most remembered today. Each householder had to register with the local

Food Office, who issued a ration book and allocated rations based on the family size. Local shopkeepers also had to register and received an allocation of rationed goods in line with the number of customers they supplied. The shopkeepers would then supply the rations to their customers, clipping the food ration coupons from their ration books. The quantity of any item allowed per person varied throughout the war according to government instructions. Many items were in short supply. Fresh eggs were replaced by egg powder, and items like sugar, tea, butter or margarine were limited to a few ounces per week. Fruit, such as oranges, bananas and lemons were rarely seen until after the war. However, Docking was fortunate to have a local baker, Mr Terence Rowland Wagg, known as 'TR' to the locals, who supplied fresh bread and pies from his shop opposite the Hare Inn. He also delivered these products to outlying areas using his small fleet of vans, even using horses when the roads were impassable because of drifting snow.

In common with most rural people, Docking's inhabitants maintained large vegetable gardens and allotments to support the government's 'Dig for Victory' campaign. Despite the fact that key agricultural workers had been given deferment from call-up, many local men volunteered or were called up into the armed services. This left the wives with most of the household duties, including the tending of gardens, allotments and domestic animals.

The villagers also kept chickens, rabbits and other animals for home-grown

meat. Rabbits were a particularly good source of food, which could be raised cheaply on garden waste, dandelion leaves and the like. Chickens, on the other hand, were generally considered too valuable to eat, because of their eggs. The alternative to fresh eggs was the much disliked egg powder. Clubs were set up to encourage the breeding of chickens and rabbits. The Docking and district Poultry and Rabbit Club was duly established and held its first meeting in 1943. Docking also had a flourishing Horticultural Society, which hosted an annual show to exhibit prized vegetables, fruit, cut flowers and plants as well as needlecraft and home-made bread and cakes. These were judged and prizes awarded in each class of exhibit. The annual Horticultural Show was usually followed by a fair and sports day for the children.

During the war years, the village did its best to raise money for local and national causes. Dances, whist drives, raffles, sales, collections, sports events and church services were devoted to raising funds. The vicar, Rev. F.G. Ward, would hold special services in the church and hope for a large congregation and good collection to bolster the village's fund raising efforts. Dances and other functions were held in the Oddfellows Hall, now known as the Dr Ripper Memorial Hall. Apart from their fund-raising potential, these dances and other social events were a great opportunity for the locals to mix with the visiting airmen and airwomen from the RAF camp. There are many references in the wartime newspapers to the fund-raising efforts of Mrs J.H.M. Hare and others, who regularly organized collections for the Lynn Hospital, Red Cross, prisoners-of-war fund and other worthy causes. Whist drives and other functions were frequently held at Mrs Hare's residence, Docking Hall. Collections would be made in the public houses in aid of various causes. Even Docking school, led by the Headmaster, Mr A.J. Spooner, entered into the fund-raising spirit of the time. Staff and scholars would undertake envelope collections for various worthy causes.

People were encouraged to save their hard-earned money in government Savings Bonds, National War Bonds, Defence Bonds or Savings Certificates, which gave a return of 2½-3% per annum. Alternatively, they could deposit their money in the Post Office Savings Bank or buy saving stamps. Savings stamps were available at 6d or 2/6d each from a post office or from local savings groups, who would conduct house-to-house canvassing. Many people now believe that the hidden purpose of national savings was to take money out of circulation and to discourage people from spending their spare cash, thus reducing the demand for goods. From today's perspective, the publicity seems to over-simplify things by suggesting that extra tanks, planes or warships would be built if people saved appropriate sums of money for that purpose Nevertheless, special savings weeks such as 'Warship Week' or 'Wings for Victory Week', would be held each year, when the village tried to maximize its savings for a particular cause. Docking Rural District Council organized paper, rubber, rags and metal salvage contests between the various villages throughout the war. The Council also organized the special savings weeks and set targets for each village in the district.

A Warship Week was held in Docking rural district from 21 to 28 February 1942, when the savings target was set at £70,000. Each village was given a target and organized its own calendar of events to raise its savings contribution. The Docking village Warship Week opened on the Saturday with a dance at the Oddfellows hall, where Miss Sylvia Groom was selected for the district's 'Miss Britannia' beauty competition. Each village selected its candidate for the 'Miss Britannia' beauty contest, to compete in the final held during another dance in the Oddfellows hall on Thursday, 26 February. Miss Groom was eventually crowned as the district's 'Miss Britannia', receiving her prize of seven savings certificates. Second and third prizes, also savings certificates, were awarded for

DOCKING RURAL
WARSHIP WEEK
WE HAVE "ONE IN MIND" which will be "ONE IN THE EYE" FOR THEM

"AN EYE FOR AN EYE" — HORATIO SAVED ALL; WE MUST ALL SAVE "OUR RATIO"! £70,000 = £4 per head

Docking Warship Week cartoon in the local papers in February 1942

the runners-up. The Rev. F. G. Ward held a united service at the parish church on the Sunday, when contingents of the RAF and Civil Defence workers paraded and attended. On Monday, a collection of model aeroplanes, ships and other exhibits were placed on view at the Oddfellows Hall, and Mrs Hare hosted a whist drive at Docking Hall. Throughout the week, the savings coordinators conducted door-to-door canvassing to encourage people to purchase savings certificates and savings stamps.

Docking district 'sponsored' a Motor Torpedo Boat (MTB) as a result of this successful 'Warship Week'. Docking RDC presented a plaque to the vessel to mark this particular event. The plaque was a replica of the Docking village sign, containing a 'V' for Victory. It was made using oak from Burnham Thorpe (Nelson's birthplace). In a letter to the Council, the Commanding Officer of the MTB acknowledged receipt of this plaque as follows:

'We sincerely hope that this emblem you have sent to us will help to tie us together with bonds as sturdy and true as the British oak from which it is made. To us it is a delight to the eye, and a symbol that behind us we have the people of this country, of village and of town, to back us up, and to provide us with the weapons with which to win this war. We are very proud of our little vessel, and we hope we shall continue to have good cause to be proud, and to make you proud.'

81

Later in the same year Docking rural district failed to reach its 'Tanks for Attack' target, when a total of only £36,599 was invested during a ten-week period against a target of over £56,000. The savings organizers were disappointed, but explained it away by reasoning that the period covered August and September, the harvest months, when country people were too busy in the fields to think about savings.

Generally, however, the district did very well during these savings 'drives'. Another successful example was the 'Wings for Victory Week' held in the period of 29 May to 5 June 1943. A district target of £60,000 was set, being the approximate cost of a Lancaster bomber plus a Mosquito aircraft. Each village was given an individual target, Docking's being £4,000 on this occasion. Each village then arranged its own set of functions and collections to raise its share of the overall target. Brancaster and Bircham opened their weeks with garden fetes, while Ingoldisthorpe began with a cricket match – Ladies versus Gentlemen.

WINGS FOR VICTORY WEEK

Let's go!

The R.A.F. wants more and more aircraft. They can't do without them. In our "Wings for Victory" Week we can show by a record savings total what we can do without to see that they get them. And to see too, that our district wins its "Victory Wings." It's no real sacrifice to save more—but, to get over our target, save more we must

May 29th - June 5th

PUT EVERYTHING INTO IT —

3% Savings Bonds
2½% National War Bonds
3% Defence Bonds
Savings Certificates
Savings Stamps
Post Office Savings Bank
Trustee Savings Bank

DOCKING R.D.

TARGET £60,000
The cost of one Lancaster and one Mosquito

At Docking this particular 'Wings for Victory Week' was opened in the grounds of Docking Hall on the Saturday. There was a march past by members of the RAF and the Commanding Officer of RAF Bircham Newton, Group Captain T.H. Carr DFC, gave an address. This was followed by an athletic display and exhibition of boxing by the RAF and a demonstration by the Home Guard. In the evening a dance was held in the Oddfellows Hall to the music of an RAF band. A unified service was held in the parish church on Sunday morning. Contingents of RAF, Home Guard and Civil Defence services paraded through Docking and were present at the service. The vicar, Rev. F.G. Ward, conducted the service, with lessons and prayers being read by the Methodist minister, Rev. A.R. Chastney. During the service, members of the Methodist choir augmented the church choir. The local Headmaster, Mr A. J. Spooner, played the church organ.

One of the strangest ways of obtaining savings stamps was offered by one frustrated gardener in the village. He offered sixpenny savings stamps for each dozen white cabbage butterflies caught by children within 200 yards of his residence. The result of his generous offer was said to have 'far exceeded expectations'.

The Docking rural district 'Wings for Victory Week' in 1943 realized more than £125,000, which was more than double the target. Docking, combined with Chosely, realized more than £5,400 against their target of £4,000. Some villages did even better, achieving

82

more than double their target figures. Mr T. A. Ringer, who was the chairman of Docking RDC, later thanked all the contributors, making special mention of the very substantial increase in the amount subscribed by small savers and to his gratitude for the assistance given by RAF personnel. This was not the only time the RAF personnel participated in a Docking event in 1943; RAF and WAAF contingents marched with the British Legion prior to the annual Remembrance Day service in November.

Docking had its share of wartime evacuees, including a complete school, called Chequer Street School, which was evacuated from East London. This school was uprooted and re-established in Docking's Methodist Chapel in 1939, complete with teachers and pupils, who lived with local families. These London evacuees were integrated into village life and mixed with the local children as much as possible. On rare occasions, the children would be treated to a film show and party in the Oddfellows Hall. Unfortunately, they didn't often get to see Tom Mix or the other cowboy heroes of the time, since the Ministry of Information produced most of the films on offer. The children returned to London in 1942, much healthier as a result of their stay in Norfolk.

Wartime Docking would have looked very drab when compared to the modern village, particularly during the hours of darkness. Blackout regulations meant that there were no street lights and thick blackout curtains prevented any light from escaping from buildings. Windows in public buildings were also taped up to prevent them from shattering in the event of a bomb blast. The roads would have been relatively quiet, except for military vehicles transporting men and equipment between the two RAF stations at Docking and Bircham Newton. Even the road signs had been removed to confuse any invading army.

Although they sported blackout curtains, and looked quite dark from the outside, the public houses, such as the Railway Inn, the Hare Inn, the Plough and the King William, provided a warm and cheery welcome inside. With the influx of RAF and WAAF personnel, the Docking pubs did a roaring trade. Local tradesmen also benefited from a larger number of customers, despite the food rationing. Terence Wagg sold bread, pies and cakes from his shop opposite the Hare Inn. Don Playford sold fish and chips, wrapped in greaseproof paper and newspaper, as was the custom at that time. Lou Bayfield and Crew Masters, sold sausages, meat and game from their butcher's shops. William Roy and Ernest Peck both prospered from sales from their stores at opposite ends of the village. Utting's ironmongers store, which sold everything from nails to broomsticks, did increased trade, especially in candles and paraffin for lamps used to illuminate many homes in those days. Even the branch of Barclay's Bank, only open on Thursdays, was probably busier than in pre-war years.

Petty sessions were held on the last Monday in each month at Docking's courthouse, called the Session house. Some of the alleged crimes committed during the wartime years seem petty in the extreme today. For example, at a time when blackout regulations were rigorously enforced, it is surprising how

83

many individuals were summoned to appear before the court for riding their bicycles without proper lights. Many punishable offences were associated with enforcing blackout regulations, including the showing of house lights during blackout periods, illuminating the road with a powerful beam from a bicycle or car light or the failure to fit hoods to car lights. Other trivial offences that took up the court's time included the possession of a dog without a license, or providing a lift on the crossbar of a bicycle.

The magistrates clearly had an increased number of cases to deal with because of the influx of service personnel. One sad case occurred in early 1943, when a young member of the WAAF appeared before the court and was bound over until August of the following year, when she would celebrate her 21st birthday. This aircraftwoman (ACW) had been working in a service Post office at an RAF station when she committed her crime. As was usual in wartime, the RAF station wasn't named, but it was probably Docking, Bircham Newton or North Creake, three RAF stations in the Docking rural district. Apparently, when investigators made a tour of inspection they found articles in the salvage box, which aroused their suspicions. The ACW admitted that sometimes parcels were broken and the goods exposed, and at other times she had opened parcels, taken out what she wanted, and wrapped them up again. Most of what she had stolen she had sent home to her mother and two sisters. She admitted stealing money, sweets, 24 bars of chocolate, food and clothing of total value £4 14s 2d. She also admitted that she failed to redirect 113 letters belonging to personnel that had been posted away from the station. Surprisingly, the chairman of the bench dealt very leniently with this case. He made allowances for the ACW's young age relative to her high responsibilities, and he concluded that she had not been properly supervised. Compare this to the punishment handed out on the same day to a Docking tractor driver, who was found guilty, heavily fined, and subsequently lost his job and his tied cottage because he was caught with a bag of corn on his back, which he had stolen from a heap on a barn floor.

At the start of the war, the government turned to the commonwealth for help in training aircrew because there were insufficient facilities in the United Kingdom and because home airfields were vulnerable to attack. A British Commonwealth Air Training Plan (BCATP) was agreed between Canada, the United Kingdom, Australia and New Zealand and more than 150 schools were established across Canada to train pilots, wireless operators, air gunners and navigators for the air forces of these nations. Thousands of air cadets were sent from the UK to train at these schools. The BCATP was terminated at the end of March 1945, and the cadets under training at that time were returned to their home countries. Since the war was coming to an end, most of them that were not required for flying duties were sent to various RAF centres awaiting demobilization. Docking became one of these holding centres, since the airfield and its accommodation were no longer required operationally.

Two ex-cadets who found themselves at Docking in 1945 were the would-be actors Richard Burton and Mick Misell (Warren Mitchell). In 1944 Richard had met fellow-student Mick when they were both studying on a six-month course at Exeter College, Oxford under an Air Ministry Training Scheme. One of the things that had drawn Richard and Mick together was a mutual love of the theatre. They subsequently joined the RAF at the same time and were selected for training as aircrew cadets in Canada (Winnipeg), returning to England in late 1945. Richard always stated that he reluctantly trained as a navigator when his eyesight was found to be inadequate for a pilot. While at Docking, from where he made frequent visits to London, Richard developed a relationship with a young actress, Eleanor Summerfield. He would use up his quota of weekend passes hitch-hiking to distant theatres following his new girlfriend, who was on tour with a theatre company. Richard was to become a household name for his many brilliant stage and screen roles and because of his stormy marriages to Elizabeth Taylor. After studying at the Royal Academy of Dramatic Art (RADA), Mick was also to carve out a distinguished career on stage and television as the actor Warren Mitchell; he is best remembered for his portrayal of the bigoted cockney, Alf Garnett, in the TV series 'Till Death Us Do Part'.

Robert (Tim) Hardy, who subsequently became famous as the actor Robert Hardy, was also at Docking with Burton for a time, until he managed to wangle a transfer to London. He regularly returned to visit Richard at Docking, where they would discuss Shakespeare and their aspirations for acting roles. Robert later admitted that Richard had got up to all sorts of mischief at Docking, and, in his words, 'sailed very close to the law'. Robert Hardy later found fame as the senior vet in the TV series 'All Creatures Great and Small' and for his many brilliant portrayals of Winston Churchill.

Derek Small, who also trained in Canada and found himself at Docking with Burton, Hardy and Misell, confirmed that they had met at Oxford University in 1944 and then joined the RAF together. They were sent to Canada for aircrew training, and on their return, were sent to Docking to await demobilization. Since Docking's operational days were over, there was little for them to do and boredom set in. To pass the time, they soon got up to all sorts of pranks. Derek remembered them drinking and singing in several local pubs, including the Railway Inn, which was a short distance from their barracks. He also remembered Docking railway station as their gateway to the outside world. There were frequent trains which allowed them access to the local towns of Hunstanton and King's Lynn. Derek could not remember much about the airfield, since he had little reason for visiting it, except to dine at the airmen's mess.

Richard Burton's memories of his time at Docking were very frank and revealing. He said that he had languished for months at Docking with nothing to do but play rugby and challenge air force rules. He played for Bircham Newton's rugby XV as a wing forward. After the games they would drink a lot and get into fights. On his twentieth birthday, in November 1945, he was said to have got very drunk with a group of wild friends, who between them smashed 17 windows by putting their fists through them. Richard later said that they were punished with seven days jankers. Apparently, an unpopular sergeant, who had tried to discipline him and his friends, was beaten up and almost died. Richard moved into Docking Hall and acted as though he were the lord of the manor gaining the nickname of 'the Squire of Docking'. From his memoirs one also has the impression that he was permanently hungry. He recalls raiding farmer's fields to get turnips, 'mangold-wurzels' and mushrooms to fry up for breakfast.

There was no real work, and so they spent their time cleaning lavatories and peeling potatoes. Burton followed girls with dedication, without emotion or remorse. He retained an insatiable thirst for women, seeming to use them to boost his own ego. From all accounts, he spent most of his time drinking, singing, bedding the local girls and getting into trouble. Moreover, after he left Docking, he was unconcerned, or unaware, that his vivid recollections might tarnish the reputation of at least one Docking girl. Mick Misell once had to impersonate Richard when asked to date one of the Welshman's many girlfriends. Apparently, he imitated Richard's Welsh accent, spouted a bit of Shakespeare and dated the unsuspecting girl for three weeks. Fortunately, before they could do too much damage, these future celebrities were released from the RAF in 1947 to pursue their acting careers.

Danny Blanchflower, later to captain Tottenham Hotspurs and Northern Ireland at football, also found himself in Docking with Richard Burton at the end of the war. Danny had followed a similar route to Richard and the others. He attended St Andrews University on a short course under the Air Ministry Training Scheme, was recommended for a commission in the RAF and sent to Canada for navigation training. However, when the war was over, he was sent home with many other cadets to await his demobilization at Docking. When home on Christmas leave from Docking at the end of 1945, he obtained his first senior debut for Glentoran, one of Northern Ireland's finest football teams. He was released from the RAF in 1946 to begin his illustrious football career, which reached a pinnacle when he captained the Spurs double-winning side in 1961.

7. Docking Airfield Today

The area around Sunderland Farm, including the main airfield sites, can be seen on this map, which was produced in 1965.

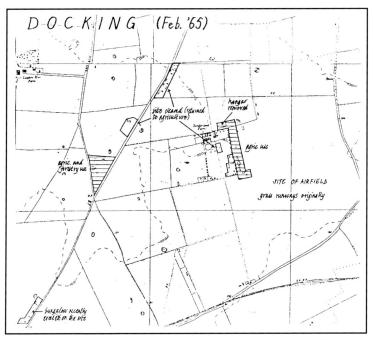

Leaving the village of Docking on the B1154, at the bottom left-hand corner of the map, the first ex-RAF site is reached within a few hundred yards on the left-hand side of the road. This site originally contained Maycrete and Nissen huts used as airmen's barracks. A modern bungalow now occupies this site, and it is almost unrecognisable as former RAF quarters. However, remains of one or two RAF huts are still visible behind the hedgerow that screens this site.

At the first fork in this road, a small wooded area has been planted with fir trees, hiding the decaying remains of two old buildings, which were a decontamination centre and the standby set house, which accommodated the standby electrical generator that would supply electrical power should there be a failure of the outside power supply. The other buildings that straddled the minor road leading away from the fork, including the Laing huts where the author lived in the late 1940s, were completely cleared some years ago and the land has been returned to agricultural use.

RAF quarters that were located at the side of the B1154 near to Lugden Hill Farm have also been cleared. Nothing remains of the hutments and air raid shelters that originally occupied these sites. Also the metal water tower and gantry that was near the junction of the minor road and the track leading to Sunderland farmhouse has disappeared, except for some concrete remains at ground level.

Docking Control Tower

Almost directly east of the aforementioned plantation, south of Sunderland Farm, is the remains of the control tower (or watch office). It is located near the southern end of the shaded area to the east of the farmhouse. The original grass airfield was located in the area between the control tower and the road leading to Burnham Market, which runs diagonally across the bottom right-hand corner of the map, turning in a northerly direction. Some of the old concrete perimeter tracks still survive and are being used as farm tracks. One or two other ex-RAF buildings are located between the control tower and Sunderland Farm. One building is believed to have been the squadron flight office and another appears to have been an agricultural plant store, where grass-cutting equipment and the like were stored.

Nearby there are also two pillboxes originally designed as part of the airfield defences. One of these pillboxes shows some damage, which may, in part, be the result of a Hampden crash that occurred on 10 October 1943. Two underground concrete air-raid shelters were also found. One is located in the central shaded area of the map, where most of the remains of airfield buildings are located; the other is located almost due south of the central shaded area, near to the Burnham Market road.

The pillbox or gunpost that may have been damaged by a Hampden on October 10 1943

88

The remains of an agricultural plant store, whose doors seem wide and tall enough for fire tenders

The War Graves at St Mary's Church, Great Bircham

The original Sunderland farmhouse was bombed and destroyed in 1941 together with an adjacent granary. The present house was rebuilt just after the war, on the site of the original farmhouse. A hangar that originally stood near the farmhouse was dismantled some years ago.

Except for some concrete rubble, there is little sign of the fuel compound and fuel storage dump, which was situated in the Technical Site. Similarly, the bomb store, which was situated near the north-east corner of the airfield, adjacent to the road leading to Burnham Market, has gone without trace. Even the railway track that passed the southern side of the airfield has disappeared.

Many of the fallen airmen are buried in the War Graves cemetery at St Mary's Church, Great Bircham, which contains a Cross of Sacrifice unveiled by King George VI in 1946.

One of the graves is that of Pilot Officer A.L. Kippen RCAF, an Observer with 407 Squadron. It contains a small plaque containing a poem written by his sister (Mrs Armstrong) just eight days before his death.

P/O Kippen was killed on 16 May 1942, when a badly damaged Hudson aircraft, returning from an attack on a German convoy, failed on the approach to landing at Docking. The aircraft crashed into a gun pit at the edge of the airfield also killing an Army AA gunner.

The words of this poignant poem are reproduced below:

'Oh England is a kindly land,
To all who travel there,
And England in the Maytime,
Lays fingers soft as air
On restless hearts that wonder,
Yet linger unaware.

And if one's heart lies lonely,
For the Maple's golden shade,
And if one listens mutely,
For a song that is not played,
Breathe gently on him England,
It was for you he stayed.'

Sources

Published books:

.   *Norfolk Airfields in the Second World War* by Graham Smith
.   *Airfields and Airstrips of Norfolk and Suffolk – Part One,* a Norfolk and Suffolk Aviation Museum Publication
.   *Action Stations: 1 Wartime Military Airfields of East Anglia 1939-1945* by Michael J.F. Bowyer
.   *Norfolk Military Airfields – An Operational Record 1913 to 1997* by Peter M. Walker
.   *Lockheed Hudson in World War II* by Andrew Hendrie
.   *Fly for their Lives* by John Chartres
.   *Rescue from the Skies – The Story of the Airborne Lifeboat* by Stephen Brewster Daniels
.   *Air-Sea Rescue in World War Two,* by Alan Rowe
.   *Norfolk Aviation Society's Norfolk Air Crashes Royal Air Force 1939–45* by Merv Hambling
0.   *Unsung Heroes of R.A.F. Air Sea Rescues,* by Stephen Brewster Daniels
1.   *Airfield Heyday* by Paul Berry
2.   *Wellington The Geodetic Giant* by Martin Bowman
3.   *Blenheim Squadrons of World War 2* by Jon Lake
4.   *Action Stations Revisited* by Michael J.F. Bowyer
5.   *Coastal Command – The Air Ministry account of the part played by Coastal Command in the Battle of the Seas 1939-1942* HMSO
6.   *Bring Back My Stringbag* by John Kilbracken
7.   *Even the Birds were Walking* by John A. Kington & Peter G. Rackliff
8.   *RAF Squadrons,* by Wing Commander C.G. Jefford MBE RAF
9.   *Attacker – The Hudson and its Flyers* by Geoffrey Jones
0.   *Richard Burton* by Paul Ferris
1.   *Rich – The Life of Richard Burton* by Melvyn Bragg
2.   *Richard Burton – A Brother Remembered* by David Jenkins
3.   *Danny Blanchflower – A Biography of a Visionary* by Dave Bowler
4.   *Military Airfields in the British Isles 1939–1945* by S. Willis and B. Hollis
5.   *A Forgotten Offensive* by Christina J.M. Goulter
6.   *Docking A Walk in Time* by Hermeina Elms and Eileen Wells
7.   *Dry Docking* by G. Hagan
8.   *Bircham Newton A Norfolk Airfield In War and Peace* by Peter B. Gunn
9.   *Canadian Squadrons in Coastal Command* by Andrew Hendrie

Newspaper articles and Internet resources:

I studied wartime newspapers, such as the *Lynn Advertiser*, which are held on film at King's Lynn public library. The following recent article was also relevant to my story:

'Ted was Dixon of Docking', written by Jo Garner for the *Lynn News* in 1992
Extracts are included by kind permission of the Editor of the *Lynn News*.

The following Internet articles also proved to be very useful:
'The War Graves of St Mary's Church, Great Bircham, Norfolk', available at http://www.bircham.bellringers.btinternet.co.uk
'History of No 304 (Polish) Squadron' by Wilhelm Ratuszynski, available at http://www.geocities.com/skrzyldla/304/304Story.html
'Part One – Meteorological Reconnaissance Pre 202 Squadron', available at http://www.202-sqn-assoc.co.uk

Photographs:

Jacklin family in 1948/49	from the author's collection
Early post-war photographs of	
Sunderland Farm and Docking airfield	courtesy of Mr Robert Perowne
521 Squadron personnel and aircraft	courtesy of Mr Les Hart and Mr Bill Davis
279 Squadron photographs	courtesy of Mr Frank Goff
Historical photographs of Docking	courtesy of Mr Tony Arter
Photographs of WAAF members Docking	courtesy of Mrs Doris Driver and Mrs Dorothy Jackson
Coloured photographs of Docking Airfield	from the author's collection
Photographs of Great Bircham War graves	from the author's collection

Other aircraft photographs came from various Internet websites and other sources. To the best of my knowledge, they are all in the public domain.

Ordnance Survey Maps

The Ordnance Survey extract used in the Prologue was reproduced by kind permission of Ordnance Survey © Crown copyright NC/2002/35371

Every effort has been made to obtain permission to use all of the material in this book, but the author apologises to anyone whose material may have inadvertently been used without prior permission. Finally, if there are any mistakes in the text, they are of my making, and I will attempt to correct them in future revisions of the book.